ALFRED
THE GREAT

POCKET
GIANTS

ALFRED
THE GREAT

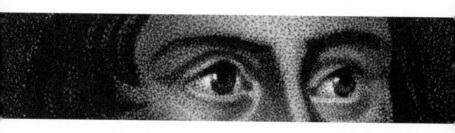

POCKET
GIANTS

BARBARA
YORKE

The
History
Press

Cover image © Bridgeman Images

First published 2015

The History Press
The Mill, Brimscombe Port
Stroud, Gloucestershire, GL5 2QG
www.thehistorypress.co.uk

British Library Cataloguing in Publication Data.
A catalogue record for this book is available from the British Library.

ISBN 978 0 7509 6147 9

Typesetting and origination by The History Press
Printed in Malta by Melita Press.

Contents

Introduction: Background and Sources

Ælfred ... is the most perfect character in history ... No other man on record has ever so thoroughly united all the virtues both of the ruler and of the private man. In no other man on record were so many virtues disfigured by so little alloy.

Edward Freeman, 1879[1]

King Alfred the Great is the most famous and celebrated of all Anglo-Saxon kings. His statue stands at the heart of a number of southern English towns – Wantage, where he was born over a thousand years ago; Winchester, where he was buried; Pewsey and Shaftesbury, where he also had strong personal connections. Other monuments to his memory can be enjoyed on a day out at Stowe Landscape Gardens, on the Stourhead estate in Wiltshire or at Athelney on the Somerset Levels. Alfred was headline news when the results of an examination of what might have been part of his skeleton were announced in Winchester. This was in January 2014, 1,115 years after his death. How has Alfred's reputation survived with such dramatic force when other powerful and high-achieving Anglo-Saxon kings have been all but forgotten? Why is he the only King of England to be known as 'the Great'?

There are three main reasons for Alfred's fame: (1) his successful defence of his kingdom against the Vikings; (2) the relatively large number of sources which survive from his reign; and (3) the desire in later centuries to find Anglo-Saxon origins for the English constitution, Church, empire and character. These three aspects coalesce so that his very real achievements have become part of a myth. It is a process that began in his lifetime and reached its apogee in the millenary celebrations of his death in 1901.

Alfred was the right person in the right place at the right time. Early in his reign he very nearly succumbed, like so many of his contemporaries, to the onslaught of the Vikings, but somehow he managed to hold out. By the time of his second campaign against the Vikings, between 892 and 896, his kingdom of Wessex was better prepared to defend itself. The military changes Alfred made saved his land and his people, and secured his reputation as a war leader. Alfred was able to leave the throne far more secure than he found it, so that his son and grandsons could in due course capitalise on his achievements to become kings of all England.

Alfred lived at the time of what is now known as the Carolingian Renaissance, a period of heightened interest in learning and the written word in western Europe. Due to this, his reign is among the best recorded of the entire Anglo-Saxon period. Alfred seems to have taken a strong personal interest in the production of texts in the English language, something which marks him out from all of the other Anglo-Saxon warrior kings. He commissioned a series of translations into Old English of key Latin texts. He also had circulated, and may have commissioned, the *Anglo-Saxon Chronicle*, which recorded, in the native tongue, the main events of his and earlier periods, beginning with the invasion of Britain by Julius Caesar in 54 BC and rapidly moving on to the arrival of the Anglo-Saxons, including Alfred's supposed ancestors Cerdic and Cynric in the fifth century.

The *Chronicle*, as we have it, consists of various manuscript versions of an original compilation made in Alfred's reign. Topics covered are limited and seem to reflect his known interests: the accessions and deaths of kings, visits by West Saxons to Rome and, above all, battles. Very unusually among contemporary writing, there is relatively little on ecclesiastical matters and nothing to associate the work with a particular religious community. Its brief and laconic entries are deceptively simple. This was a collection of material carefully chosen to show Alfred in a favourable light.

The first stage of compilation was completed sometime between 890 and 892, when Alfred was about 40 years of age and had been on the throne for some two decades. It was probably circulated when it was apparent that another major round of Viking wars was starting. The entries for this second phase of war are considerably more detailed, perhaps made soon after they took place, and give us much information about ninth-century military manoeuvres. These entries may have been distributed as a 'top-up' to those places which had received a copy of the main *Chronicle* compilation.

Most crucial of all for Alfred's subsequent reputation was the Latin biography written by one of his court advisers, the Welsh scholar monk Asser, who eventually became one of the bishops of Wessex. The *Life of Alfred*, written in 893 while the king was still alive, is the only biography that survives for an Anglo-Saxon king and provides types of information about the man and his reign that we do not have for other pre-Norman rulers. A translation of the *Anglo-Saxon Chronicle* forms the main structure of the narrative, together with some additional information which may have come from the recollections of the king himself or other war veterans at his court. On to this framework Asser pastes other information and vignettes in rough chronological sequence. There are scenes from Alfred's childhood, his interest in learning, the illnesses from which he suffered, his religious attitudes and his concerns with the operation of law, together with various observations about his position as king. It seems to offer insight into the king's innermost thoughts. But caution is necessary. Asser's work is far from an objective critique of the king and his reign. It is clearly framed in terms of contemporary ideals of kingship, based on classical, biblical and Frankish prototypes, to which his Alfred is made to conform. The *Life* has to be seen alongside the work of other court scholars who helped make the translations of Latin works into Old English during Alfred's reign. We have a relatively clear idea of what this coterie of churchmen considered to be the qualities of an ideal ruler. There is a strong influence from the land of Francia, across the Channel, from works produced at the courts of the great kings Charlemagne (Charles the Great, d. 814), his son Louis the Pious (d. 840) and grandsons Lothair (d. 855), Louis the German (d. 876) and Charles the Bald (d. 877) – the last was Alfred's step-grandfather.

How far Alfred himself subscribed to their interpretation of kingship is a crucial matter on which it is possible to take divergent views. Asser's biography was never widely circulated under the king's imprimatur in the way that the *Anglo-Saxon Chronicle* seems to have been. This could be an indication that Alfred did not fully condone its contents, that it was not how he wanted posterity to remember him. The work may never even have been completed. It lacks a conclusion, and there are evident minor errors and places where it appears that more information was to be inserted at some future date. It is dedicated to Alfred, but in it Asser often seems to be addressing his fellow countrymen in Wales. One theory is that it was begun when Alfred needed to encourage the Welsh kingdoms into a political alliance, and abandoned when the diplomatic situation subsequently changed.

Although the *Life* was not widely circulated, it was known to later medieval historians such as William of Malmesbury (d. *c.* 1143) and Henry of Huntingdon (d. *c.* 1157), who wrote about the Anglo-Saxon past. They summarised what Asser had said, and they added in further information on Alfred's reign, some deriving from oral tradition and some of it mere inference. As Asser provided their template, a very positive portrait of the king was passed on to subsequent ages. When churchmen and politicians in later centuries wanted to discover Anglo-Saxon precedents for their own activities, it was Asser's *Life of King Alfred* and its later accretions which came most conveniently to hand. Asser would have considered it a job well done when the Victorian historian Edward Freeman declared Alfred to have been 'the most perfect character in history'.[2]

There is, therefore, a considerable challenge for the modern historian in knowing how far to trust what Asser has to say about Alfred. The *Life* undoubtedly preserves important details, but some of the seductive vignettes Asser provides prove insubstantial on close examination. For instance, Asser describes how Alfred's mother promised a book of Anglo-Saxon poetry to whichever of her sons could recite its contents to her first.[3] Alfred learned the poems by heart when someone read them to him, and so beat his four older brothers to the prize. However, Alfred was only an infant when his mother died, while his oldest brothers were grown men who were unlikely to want to be involved in competitive poetry reciting. Can we really believe that this incident actually happened? Various apparent errors, such as in names of individuals or dates, make one wonder if Asser was actually as close to Alfred and the affairs of the court as he tries to imply.

An extreme reaction to the suspicion that many of Asser's stories were fabrications led the historian Alfred Smyth in 1995 to declare that Asser's *Life* was a forgery written in eastern England in the tenth century.[4] It is a view not generally accepted by historians today, but it does point to the fact that there was a process of Alfredian myth-making at work. Parallels with the exemplary kings of the Old Testament, especially David and Solomon, often underpin the depictions of Alfred. When Asser writes of Alfred carefully dividing his revenues into equal fractions for various types of expenditure, or ingeniously designing a candle clock, one has to appreciate that there are close similarities to the portrayal of King Solomon in the Old Testament.[5]

So can we get behind Asser's idealised portrait to catch a glimpse of the real King Alfred? Our quest is made all the harder by the fact that the majority of sources which survive from Alfred's reign, probably including the *Anglo-Saxon Chronicle*, were produced by the same scholarly circle to which Asser belonged. They shared the same ideals and the same sense of purpose – which included wanting to persuade the king to listen to what they had to say. Fortunately, a few other unrelated documents also survive, including King Alfred's will, his law code and letters. In them the king can be seen in a less idealised light. Archaeological evidence and artefacts such as coins and the Alfred Jewel provide another way of assessing the portrait produced by his scholarly advisers. It may be impossible to recover fully the 'real' Alfred, but we can strip away some of the myth to reveal a more realistic king in his historical context – less the idealised Christian ruler, and more the shrewd, battle-hardened warrior.

By the time Alfred came to the throne in 871, Anglo-Saxons had been living in Britain for over 300 years. They came originally from lands across the North Sea, from what is now Germany and Denmark, first to raid and then, after the Roman legions left Britannia, to establish permanent bases on the island. By the seventh century various small Anglo-Saxon kingdoms had begun to emerge, especially in the south and east of England. Their kings seem to have welcomed Christianity as part of the stabilisation of their power and were particularly proud to be associated with a mission sent by Pope Gregory the Great from Rome in the year 597.

Our main source of evidence for this period is the *Ecclesiastical History of the English People* completed by the scholar monk Bede in about 731. From the perspective of those living in the ninth century the world of Bede appeared to be something of a golden age – a time when, to cite a letter sent by Alfred to his bishops, kings 'maintained their peace, morality and authority at home but also extended their territory outside; and ... succeeded both in warfare and in wisdom'.[6] Such a vision of stability and order was illusory, but it provided an ideal towards which Alfred's court could aspire. One of the first works translated by the king and his court scholars was the *Pastoral Care* of Pope Gregory the Great, to which Alfred's letter formed a preface.

By the end of the seventh century some of the central Anglo-Saxon settlements had grown substantially by extending westwards. The four major kingdoms were Northumbria, East Anglia, Mercia (the Midlands) and Wessex (Hampshire westwards, south of the Thames) (see Maps). Northumbria was the great power of the first half of the seventh century, after which Mercia became increasingly powerful and dominated in the eighth. King

Offa of Mercia (757–96), a contemporary of Charlemagne, was particularly expansionist and quickly incorporated a number of small kingdoms in the east and south.

When Alfred was born in 848/49 there were still four Anglo-Saxon kingdoms. But by the time of his death in 899 Wessex was the only one surviving intact with its own Anglo-Saxon royal house. The story of Alfred's reign is not just about how Wessex was able to continue when the other kingdoms fell to the Vikings, but how Alfred managed to ensure that his successors went on to become kings of all England – that is, rulers over all the former kingdoms of Mercia, East Anglia and Northumbria as well as Wessex.

1

Family and Childhood, 848/49–71

Now, he was greatly loved, more than all his brothers, by his father and mother – indeed, by everybody – with a universal and profound love … As he passed through infancy and boyhood he was seen to be more comely in appearance than his brothers, and more pleasing in manners, speech and behaviour.

Asser, 893[7]

Alfred was born on a royal estate at Wantage in Oxfordshire. The year is given as 849 by Asser, but information in the *Anglo-Saxon Chronicle* suggests either 847 or 848. Alfred was the youngest of the six children – five sons and a daughter – of King Æthelwulf (839–58) and his wife Osburh, a West Saxon noblewoman (see Family Tree). There were several rival royal lines in Wessex. Alfred's branch had only occasionally dominated the kingship, though he could trace his lineage to the brother of one of the most significant earlier kings, Ine (688–725). It was Alfred's grandfather Ecgbert (802–39) who had changed the family's fortunes in a spectacular way. He had been able to take advantage of the declining power of the previously dominant midland kingdom of Mercia to take control of its lands in the south-east of Kent, Sussex and Essex. From the time of Ecgbert Wessex consisted of all England south of the Thames plus Essex. Wantage, where Alfred was born, lay close to the northern border of Wessex and had only recently been taken back from Mercia.

We know next to nothing of the childhood of most Anglo-Saxon kings, but Alfred (thanks to Asser) is an exception. His early years were full of incident. By the time he was 5 or 6 he had lost his mother and gained a stepmother, been to Rome twice and witnessed a coup by one of his brothers against their father.

Æthelwulf's decision to send his youngest son (and possibly also the one next in age to him, Æthelred) to Rome in 853 is hard to fathom. Rome was an unhealthy place and the journey was long and arduous – King Ine had died on a visit there in 725, and in 958 an archbishop-elect of Canterbury froze to death in the Alps en route from the Holy See. Perhaps Æthelwulf had hoped to make the pilgrimage himself, but sent Alfred instead as the family representative, while he fended off Viking attacks at home. When Æthelwulf did eventually manage to make the journey to the centre of Western Christendom a couple of years later, he took Alfred with him. On their way back in 856 they stopped for several months at the court of Charles the Bald, grandson of the Emperor Charlemagne, mighty ruler of western Francia (see Family Tree). There Æthelwulf, who was probably in his 50s by this time, married Charles's 12-year-old daughter, Judith. Marriage into the premier royal family of western Europe was a major achievement for the much smaller and poorer West Saxon kingdom and probably sealed a pact between the two provinces against their mutual Viking enemies.

Before leaving for Rome, Æthelwulf had divided control of his kingdom between his two oldest surviving sons (their elder brother Athelstan had died sometime between 851 and 854). The senior of the two, Æthelbald, was given responsibility for the main part of the West

Saxon kingdom, while his brother Æthelbert supervised the more recently acquired lands in the south-east.

Once established in power, Æthelbald and his advisers indicated that they were not prepared to allow Æthelwulf to return. Perhaps Æthelbald had not expected his father to survive the trip to Rome. Perhaps he feared for his position as heir-apparent if Æthelwulf had more sons by his prestigious and young second wife. There was a real possibility of civil war, but a compromise was brokered whereby Æthelwulf agreed to return merely as king of the south-eastern provinces of Wessex, leaving his oldest son as ruler of the main part of the kingdom. When Æthelwulf died in 858, Æthelbert resumed control of the south-eastern provinces – and Æthelbald married Judith (perhaps the alliance with western Francia was too important to pass up). He did not, however, enjoy his new status or his new wife for long as he died shortly thereafter. Alfred's three brothers who ruled before him all had short reigns, but there is no evidence about the circumstances surrounding their deaths.

From what we know of his will, it seems to have been Æthelwulf's intention that Æthelred and then Alfred would succeed Æthelbald, with Æthelbert remaining in charge of the south-eastern areas – presumably as an independent kingdom. But Æthelred and Alfred were still too young to rule in their own right in 860, so Æthelbert succeeded to the whole of Wessex. When he died in 865, he was followed by Æthelred. Alfred in turn succeeded Æthelred in 871, apparently just as their father had intended.

These early and formative experiences of travel, not to mention the tumultuous toing and froing of the crown of Wessex, must have had a profound impact on the young Alfred. The feeling that he had a special relationship with Rome seems to have remained with him throughout his life, and in his later years he corresponded with popes and sent regular alms payments to Rome. It is clear that he also wanted to bring aspects of the culture and learning of the Frankish world to Wessex, not only as a result of his stay there, but perhaps also because of the influence of his young stepmother, who may have supervised his upbringing to at least 858. She was, after all, much closer in age to the young prince than she was to his father.

Asser was outraged by Æthelbald's coup and marriage to Judith:

> Once King Æthelwulf was dead, Æthelbald his son, against God's prohibition and Christian dignity, and also contrary to the practice of all pagans, took over his father's marriage-bed and married Judith, daughter of Charles [the Bald], king of the Franks, incurring great disgrace from all who heard of it.[8]

As a churchman he would have seen the marriage of a son to his father's widow as scandalous and against Christian custom. Perhaps he was also reflecting the views of Alfred. The more formal record of the *Anglo-Saxon Chronicle* does not acknowledge that Æthelbald began ruling before his father died. Only a close reading of a list of West Saxon kings and the years they reigned confirms Asser's account that Æthelbald had taken the throne prematurely. As we might expect, the sympathies of Alfred's court were firmly with Æthelwulf.

We have only limited information about Alfred between 858 and the accession of his brother Æthelred in 865. Asser tells us that he had learned to read Old English by the age of 12, and particularly valued traditional poems – probably those which celebrated the great Germanic heroes of the past:[9] *Beowulf* with its tales of monster- and dragon-slaying is the best-known example. In later life Alfred apparently lamented that he had not received a more scholarly education. The emphasis was on developing his skills as a warrior. Asser tells us that hunting was one of the skills in which the young Alfred excelled as part of his training for the realities of war.

Asser provides only one real sidelight on Alfred as an adolescent, and this concerns some mysterious illnesses.[10] Asser tells us that, disturbed by lustful thoughts, the young Alfred prayed for an illness to distract him. (The sowing of wild oats is a distinct possibility, and there is even a putative candidate for an illegitimate son of Alfred.)[11] Alfred's request was rewarded with what Asser called *ficus*, something fig-like, perhaps a growth of some kind or a particularly nasty attack of haemorrhoids (all that horse-riding). As always, one should be careful what one wishes for, and Alfred found that although his lust abated, so too did his ability to carry out his public duties. On a hunting trip in Cornwall he prayed at the shrine of St Guerir for a less severe and less visible disease. In 868, when he was approaching 20, he experienced the first of a severe series of abdominal pains which were to recur throughout his life and leave him temporarily incapacitated. For maximum embarrassment, the first attack occurred in the midst of the celebrations of his wedding to Ealhswith, a well-connected Mercian noblewoman. Doctors at the time do not seem to have known exactly what the trouble was, and neither do we – some people assumed it was the result of witchcraft. A putative diagnosis of Crohn's disease is often suggested, but this would surely have been too severe a malady for Alfred to have coped with in the absence of modern medicine.

How historians have responded to the accounts of Alfred's illnesses provides something of a touchstone for their attitudes to the king and to Asser as a source of information. Some have refused to believe that a king who achieved so much could have suffered serious illness, and they have accused Asser of exaggeration. Others have seen it as confirmation that the *Life* was a later forgery. Yet others – especially in the nineteenth century when people often had to carry on as best they could with all sorts of afflictions – regarded the illnesses as a realistic and indeed inspiring aspect of the king's character.

Recent commentary has provided more nuanced analysis of what might have been an early medieval churchman's understanding of illness. Asser saw such tribulations as a sign from God.[12] Just as Christ had been pierced on the Cross, so the illness which afflicted

Alfred was one of several 'nails' (along with Viking raids and disobedient subjects) he had to endure. As a king on earth he suffered so that his subjects did not have to. The implication was that he should therefore receive from them the type of respect and obedience accorded to the King of Heaven. Such an interpretation, written in 893, boosted Alfred's esteem while helping to nudge the king in the direction that his advisers wished him to go in order to fulfil their programme of Christian rule. Back in 868, however, the young Alfred must have struggled to make sense of what was happening to him.

Whatever the nature of his illness, it did not prevent Alfred from siring five children: two sons and three daughters. Asser says that there were a number of others who died in infancy.[13] The oldest child was a girl, Æthelflaed, who went on to marry Æthelred of Mercia in 886 or 887, and – remarkably – took over his role when he died and led Mercian forces in battle. Next came a second daughter, Æthelgifu, who as a young teenager became abbess of Shaftesbury in Dorset, a nunnery founded by King Alfred. His son Edward, who was to succeed him, seems to have been close in age to the third daughter Ælfthryth, and the two were raised together at the royal court. Ælfthryth would make a diplomatic marriage towards the end of Alfred's reign with the count of Flanders (who was the son of Alfred's stepmother Judith by a third marriage). The youngest was Æthelweard, of whom little is known except that he had two sons, died in 920 and is buried in Winchester.

We have only scant insight into the marriage of Alfred and Ealhswith. Asser scarcely alludes to her and never even mentions her by name. We know little more than that she had an estate in Winchester which became a nunnery after Alfred's death and that she possessed a prayer book which survives to this day and can be seen in the British Library.[14] It was quite normal in the early Middle Ages for a king's widow to retire to a nunnery after her husband's death, though Ealhswith only survived Alfred by two years. It can at least be said that Alfred remained with Ealhswith, even after she passed childbearing age. This was by no means always the case. Alfred's son Edward was to have three wives, and one of Edward's grandsons married three times before dying in his early thirties. Some queens probably died in childbirth, but others had to withdraw to nunneries to allow the kings to remarry. Perhaps Alfred was affected by the experience of his early illness and the lessons his religious advisers drew from it about the necessity of continence in marriage, especially for godly kings.

Asser's account of Alfred's childhood is suffused with the idea of a young prince born to rule. Asser does not miss a chance to emphasise that Alfred was more skilled and accomplished than his older brothers, better at hunting, better at learning poetry by heart and better loved by his parents and by the people, as the quotation at the head of this chapter shows.

The *Anglo-Saxon Chronicle* records that in 853 the Pope had crowned the 4- or 5-year-old Alfred as king.

In fact a fragment of a surviving letter from the Pope to Alfred's father makes clear that he had merely accorded him a ceremony that made him an honorary consul.[15] Alfred's memory of what happened when he was so young may have been hazy, but it must have suited him to stress that his father had always intended him to be king. Such a destiny would have seemed unlikely in 853, but by the time of his last surviving brother's death in 871 there was no realistic alternative. Although Æthelred had two sons, neither was old enough to rule – especially given the military emergency in that year. But when the *Chronicle* was being compiled and Asser was producing his biography in the early 890s the question of the succession after Alfred's death must have been a major issue. Alfred's son Edward was reaching an age when he was grown-up enough to rule. But should he be preferred to his older cousins, the sons of Æthelred? The portrayal of Alfred's childhood was strongly coloured by such concerns. As far as Asser was concerned, the child was father to the man – or at least the type of man he and his fellow advisers wanted future generations to remember.

2

King Alfred's First Viking Wars, 868–78

878. In this year in midwinter after twelfth night the enemy army came stealthily to Chippenham, and occupied the land of the West Saxons ... and the people submitted to them, except King Alfred. He journeyed in difficulties through the woods and fen-fastnesses with a small force.

Anglo-Saxon Chronicle

Viking attacks on Wessex began towards the end of the eighth century. They took the form of hit-and-run raids, targeting vulnerable religious and trading communities on the coast, such as the West Saxon trading centre of Hamwic (Southampton). Rarely did they cause problems further inland – at first. But, as the Viking fleets grew larger so did their capacity to do damage and to demand the payment of tributes.

The part of Wessex most affected initially was Kent, the first port of call for the raiding fleets as they swept in from their bases across the North Sea. As the ninth century progressed, the entire coast of Wessex became vulnerable to attack, and even its western regions were open to raids from Norse colonies in Ireland.

In 838 Alfred's grandfather Ecgbert won a notable victory over a large Viking and Cornish fleet – the latter only recently incorporated into Wessex and eager to reclaim their independence. In 851 King Æthelwulf and his son Æthelbald inflicted a significant defeat on an invading force of 350 ships which had already vanquished the King of Mercia. But in 855, the year Æthelwulf and Alfred went to Rome, there was an ominous new development – a Viking fleet overwintered in Kent for the first time.

The Vikings have a formidable reputation today as the supreme warriors of early medieval Europe. In Clive Donner's 1969 film *Alfred the Great* they are presented as professional soldiers, in contrast to the West Saxon army, which appears to be largely made up of peasants. This was far from being the case. War was as much a profession for Anglo-Saxons of a certain status as it was for the Vikings, and they trained for it from an early age. The kings of Wessex were expected to lead from the front, with the aid of ealdormen who commanded the units drawn from the different shires into which the land was divided. The West Saxons were more than capable of taking on and defeating large fleets of Viking attackers in set battle. The problem was that they had to defend a large area inhabited by many non-combatants against battle-hardened men who were intensely focused and had nothing to lose – adventurers drawn principally from Scandinavia but probably reinforced by opportunists from other parts of Europe.

The differences in war technique between Anglo-Saxons and Vikings were minor. A greater distinction was that the Anglo-Saxons were Christian whereas most Scandinavians were not. This proved highly significant, not least to those who produced our written sources. Religious houses were seen as fair game for attack by the Vikings, something which naturally horrified churchmen such as Asser, who continually refers to the Vikings as 'heathens'. It was an aspect of vulnerability for the Saxons. It did, however, provide a rallying point for the Christians of Britain against a common enemy.

The first record of Alfred fighting against the Vikings occurs after the accession of Æthelred in 865, when he would have been in his late teens; it was quite normal for early medieval princes to take a leading role in the fighting while still young. In 866 there was a disturbing new development when what became known as the 'Great Army' arrived in East Anglia, apparently with the intention of staying in England and taking over the Anglo-Saxon kingdoms. In 867 it captured much of Northumbria and killed its kings. In 868 a combined Mercian and West Saxon army force was sufficiently formidable to persuade the Great Army to come to terms at Nottingham rather than fight, but then the Vikings defeated and killed King Edmund of the East Angles (subsequently St Edmund) in 870 and conquered his kingdom. In 871 they turned their attention to Wessex. This single year saw nine major battles in Wessex and many lesser engagements. The two sides were evidently evenly matched and neither was able to win a conclusive encounter, though Æthelred and Alfred had a major victory at Ashdown on the Berkshire Downs.

Ashdown seems to have been a significant battle for Alfred, as Asser adds considerable detail to the *Anglo-Saxon Chronicle*'s short account.[16] According to his report, the West Saxon forces were split between the two brothers, each of them leading their own shield wall against the enemy. Alfred and his contingent reached the battlefield before that of his brother, who was still in his tent hearing Mass. Alfred therefore found himself in the awkward position of having either to withdraw or to engage the Vikings before his brother and his forces were in place. He chose the latter course 'acting courageously, like a wild boar'. Alfred's youthful heroics might have ended up costing the West Saxons dearly, but, as Asser records, God was on their side and after much hard fighting and many dead Vikings the brothers (Æthelred had joined by this time) were victorious. Asser's account thus stresses two of the characteristics which he identified as underpinning good early medieval kingship – bravery in battle and recognition of the need for God's support – but here divides them between the two brothers rather than projecting both on to Alfred.

In spite of this success, Alfred and Æthelred were defeated at Basing (Hampshire) a mere fortnight later. Just before Easter (15 April), Viking reinforcements arrived, and then, shortly after the festival, King Æthelred died. Possibly he died of wounds (at his burial place at Wimborne in Dorset he was regarded in the later Middle Ages as a martyr of the heathen Vikings) but none of the contemporary sources gives the cause of his death. A hiatus in rule at such a critical juncture could have been fatal, but as Alfred was already in command of part of the West Saxon army, his succession was relatively smooth, though not necessarily uncontentious. A month after Æthelred's death Alfred had to face the Vikings with a reduced army, which may suggest that not everyone was fully behind him; some may have supported the succession of his young nephews, the sons of Æthelred. Alfred failed to win a decisive victory and the *Chronicle* records that he made peace with the Vikings – which probably means he paid them a large sum to go away.

Alfred must have known it was only a matter of time before the enemy army would return to Wessex. In 874 Vikings moved their attention to Mercia and drove out its king, Burgred, Alfred's brother-in-law. This made Alfred the only Anglo-Saxon king still ruling in England. Could he survive where the others had failed?

In 876 a Viking army led by Guthrum and two allies invaded Wessex. Alfred was unable to prevent them occupying Wareham (Dorset) in the heart of his kingdom. The *Chronicle* tries to make the best of it. It records that the Vikings gave Alfred high-status hostages and swore an oath on 'the holy ring' (perhaps one of their own sacred objects), 'a thing which they would not do before for any nation'. They apparently swore that they would leave the kingdom. Instead they stole away, under cover of darkness, to Exeter, where they could entrench themselves behind its Roman walls for the winter.

The following year could have been fatal to Alfred's cause – a fleet of Viking reinforcements sailed to join their comrades in Exeter. But a sudden storm intervened, damaging or destroying 120 Viking ships moored off Swanage. After this the balance of power tipped decisively in favour of the West Saxons for a short time. The Vikings agreed to all of Alfred's demands in return for being allowed to withdraw from Exeter. Unfortunately for Alfred, they only withdrew as far as Mercia, where they implemented an agreement already reached with its new king Ceolwulf under which Ceolwulf surrendered the eastern part of his kingdom to them.

Then, in 878, soon after twelfth night, some of the same Vikings, under the command of Guthrum, 'stealthily', as the *Chronicle* puts it, crossed from Mercia into northern Wiltshire. No precise information is given, but it appears that a significant proportion of the West Saxon people submitted to the Vikings. Alfred, who seems to have been caught completely off guard by this attack outside the normal campaigning season, was forced to go into hiding at Athelney in the Somerset Levels. 'He journeyed in difficulties through the woods and fen-fastnesses with a small force,' says the *Chronicle*. The fenlands containing Athelney, 'the island of the princes', were an ideal hiding place, difficult to penetrate for those such as Guthrum who did not know the lie of the land (perhaps its was somewhere Alfred had gone hunting wildfowl when he was a boy). Asser indicates the seriousness of Alfred's predicament when he adds that the king had to support himself by raiding not only the Vikings but also the West Saxons who had submitted to them; in other words he was living something of the life of a Viking himself. Neither Asser nor the *Chronicle* gives much away about this period, but later sources make up for it by defining this as the most dramatic phase of his entire reign and the period around which later legends – the cake-burning, the visit from St Cuthbert, the secret mission to the enemy camp disguised as a minstrel – all came together.

Some historians have questioned whether Alfred was ever in quite such dire straits as is commonly thought. But it is surely taking the detection of propaganda too far to suggest that the authors of the *Chronicle* reduced Alfred to a fugitive state simply for dramatic effect, so that they could provide him with an even more triumphant return. Although none of the legends was recorded until many years after the king's death, they seem to have had their roots in stories that circulated orally about the king's near-miraculous retrieval of the situation. Alfred later founded a monastery at Athelney, and this surely suggests thanksgiving for protection and recovery when all was nearly lost.

Alfred was not, however, a forlorn deserter, alone in the marshes, as depicted in the *Life of St Neot*. He had his own household troops with him and the support of the ealdorman of Somerset with his shire levies. The ealdorman of Devon and his forces made an important intervention when they prevented another Viking force from joining up with Guthrum's army. So, by May, Alfred was able to summon sufficient forces to regroup and take on Guthrum in a set-piece battle at Edington (Wiltshire). At an appointed time fighters from Somerset, Wiltshire and Hampshire, probably alerted by messengers, assembled on the shire borders at a place called Egbert's Stone, presumably named after Alfred's famous grandfather. 'And they rejoiced to see him,' says the *Chronicle*, echoing the words used after the return of Æthelwulf following Æthelbald's coup in 858.

Two days later battle was joined. Asser provides what details we have of the fighting, and, of course, he had ample opportunity to talk to veterans, including Alfred himself. Like most battles of the period, it was fought on foot with the two sides forming walls of interlocking shields from which they shoved and hacked at the opposition. It was a lengthy affair, but in the end the Viking shield wall collapsed and Alfred and his forces pursued and cut down many of the enemy in flight. The survivors took refuge in a stronghold, where they were immediately besieged by Alfred's forces. After two weeks without adequate supplies and no hope of escape, Guthrum surrendered.

Rather than taking a savage revenge upon his captive, Alfred used his advantage to form a new alliance. No one was in any doubt about who was the senior partner. One of Alfred's conditions was that Guthrum and thirty of his chief men should be baptised as Christians. Alfred himself stood as Guthrum's godfather, sealing the new bonds between them, and Guthrum took the baptismal name of 'Athelstan', the name of Alfred's eldest brother. Several different ceremonies were involved, spread over several days. Alfred feasted his new allies and gave them generous gifts. He may have been drawing on Frankish examples in making conversion part of the peace terms with Vikings, but there were Anglo-Saxon precedents too. Feasting and gift-giving were part of the language of power and fealty in the early Middle Ages, as understood by both Anglo-Saxons and Vikings, and helped forge new obligations and relationships. Guthrum withdrew from Wessex to rule as king in East Anglia, at the same time recognising Alfred's overlordship.

Alfred had defeated Guthrum and made an ally of him, but the Viking problem was far from solved. Not only were many Viking groups settled in eastern England, there were other bands operating in France and the Low Countries who might cross over the Channel at any time. One raiding party overwintered at Fulham in 879, but returned to Francia the following spring. In 882 Alfred intercepted and defeated four ships of raiders. In 885 Alfred had to take his army into Kent to relieve a Viking siege of Rochester and send a naval force to counter another Viking raid. He had to be on his guard constantly and needed to keep the kingdom in readiness for further attacks.

Alfred had proved himself as a military commander and appeared to inspire confidence in his men so that they would rally to him even when he was in difficulties. But there were undoubtedly lessons to be learned from these first Viking wars. The English had been caught off guard in 878 without sufficient forces in the field to take on the Viking incursion immediately. Alfred had been wrong-footed in 876 and 877 as well, when the Vikings had been able to get into Wareham and Exeter and use their defensive circuits to hold out against the king. His solution was to set up a network of fortified sites known as burhs. Some were established in places that already had fortifications – like the former Roman towns of Winchester and Exeter. Others, such as the big forts at Wallingford and Cricklade, were newly built to guard crossing-points on the Thames.

The concept of burhs was not a completely new one. Mercia already had a similar defensive tradition, and use had been made of fortresses in Wessex before Alfred's succession. What was different was that Alfred instigated a much more co-ordinated system. Garrisons were stationed in the burhs, drawn from the surrounding countryside, and there was a circuit of defended sites ranged at regular intervals around the whole of Wessex, with vulnerable points covered along the coast or at river crossings. Wherever the Vikings turned up in the future there would be a force that could intercept them or prevent them occupying existing fortresses into which valuable commodities and food could be moved. These arrangements are described in a document called the Burghal Hidage, which gives a list of the burhs with an assessment in hides, the Anglo-Saxon measure of land, indicating the length of wall to be defended through public service obligations.[17] The effectiveness of burhs was demonstrated in 885 when the Anglo-Saxons inside Rochester were able to keep the attacking Viking forces at bay until Alfred was able to relieve them at the head of the main army.

Alfred was not solely concerned with military matters. The numismatic evidence suggests that he found time to improve the coinage and bring up its weight of silver following a period of debasement in earlier reigns. Nor did he set up burhs as purely defensive sites. Many of the larger ones became centres of royal administration and trade, making a significant contribution to royal revenues.

To help preserve the country from future Viking attacks, Alfred had to go far beyond mere military strategy and tactics. He had to deepen the bonds between himself and his subjects, form alliances with other rulers and, perhaps most important of all, make a royal vow to the Christian God.

3

The Years of Reconstruction, 878–92 (1): Relations with Other Kingdoms

[After he had been] showered with extravagant gifts, Anarawd ap Rhodri subjected himself with all his people to King Alfred's lordship on the same condition as Æthelred and the Mercians, namely that in every respect he would be obedient to the royal will.

Asser, 893[18]

The Anglo-Saxons had a tradition of great military overlord kings. The *Anglo-Saxon Chronicle* for 829 reproduced a list of these mighty rulers from Bede's *Ecclesiastical History* (731) and proudly added to it the name of Alfred's grandfather Ecgbert as *bretwalda*. Alfred, too, can be seen as a great overlord who exercised authority over lesser rulers beyond the boundaries of Wessex, and many of the methods he used to underpin his position were those adopted by his illustrious predecessors.

Alfred acknowledged Guthrum, after his baptism, as king in East Anglia. In exchange Guthrum recognised Alfred's overlordship. As a sign of their connection, coins were minted to Alfred's design in Guthrum's baptismal name of Athelstan. Alfred seems to have made no attempt to try to restore the Anglo-Saxon royal house of the East Angles, even though Eadwold, the brother of its last, murdered king, Edmund, was exiled in Wessex. When support came from East Anglia for the Viking fleet attacking Rochester in 885, Alfred immediately sent a naval force from Kent to exact revenge; such insubordination from a client kingdom could not be tolerated without loss of face. Just how closely Alfred and Guthrum worked together after Edington is an interesting question.

After his baptism Guthrum did not immediately retire to East Anglia. Instead he occupied the Mercian centre of Cirencester for a year. By the end of that time the Mercian king Ceolwulf II had vanished, never to be heard of again. Had Alfred and Guthrum colluded in his removal? A treaty between them survives, but can only be dated to some point between 878 and 890. It divides the spoils of Ceolwulf's disappearance between them, with a line running from the rivers Ouse and Lea via Watling Street separating an enlarged East Anglia from the southern and western parts of Mercia – which seem to have come under Alfred's overlordship (see Maps).[19]

The West Saxon royal house had been working on increasing its influence within Mercia throughout the ninth century. The importance of Ecgbert's overlordship there in 829 had led to his being described as *bretwalda* in the *Chronicle*, but the large midland kingdom was not easily subdued, and in the middle decades of the ninth century Wessex and Mercia grew to have a more equal relationship. They had a monetary alliance, with the kings of each province issuing silver coins in their own names, of similar design and weight standard. They also supported each other against the Vikings, as in 868 when Alfred and his brother King Æthelred went with an army to assist King Burgred of Mercia in the siege of Nottingham.

Marriages helped to seal the alliance. Burgred married Alfred's sister Æthelswith in 853, and Alfred's own marriage to Ealhswith in 868 was part of the same plan. Ealhswith's mother Eadburh was of royal descent – she bears the same name as the late eighth-century queen of Wessex, the daughter of the great King Offa – and her male relatives were important in royal administration as ealdormen.

The balance of power between the two provinces shifted, however, when Viking forces occupied the eastern part of Mercia after the flight of Burgred in 874. Ceolwulf II, his successor, reached an accommodation with the Vikings which meant that he was king only in the southern and western parts of Mercia. When Ceolwulf vanished, probably in 879, the Mercians had no choice but to move into a closer position of dependence upon Wessex to avoid being picked off in further Viking attacks.

The new controller of Mercia was Æthelred. His background is unknown. In West Saxon sources he is always referred to as 'ealdorman', thus underlining his dependent status, but in Mercian and Welsh sources he is sometimes referred to as 'king'. Æthelred could make grants of land without reference to Alfred, but, unlike Guthrum, it seems he was not permitted to issue currency in his own right. Coins from the Mercian centres of Oxford and Gloucester were produced in the name of Alfred, identical in form to those from West Saxon mints. Æthelred was drawn closer to the West Saxon royal house by his marriage, probably in 886 or 887, to Alfred's oldest child, Æthelflaed. Other Mercians influential at Alfred's court included Waerferth, Bishop of Worcester – who provided several priests for the royal household, as well as forming part of his circle of scholarly advisers – and Plegmund, who was appointed Archbishop of Canterbury in 890.

Kings of southern Wales also sought Alfred's protection and overlordship in the face not just of Viking threats but of potential incursions by Æthelred of Mercia and the kings of Gwynedd in North Wales. It may have been in the context of these negotiations that Alfred first met or heard about Asser from the kingdom of Dyfed, for he summoned the monk in 885 and subsequently invited him to join the group of scholarly advisers he was assembling at his court – which he did permanently from 887.[20]

Asser's biography of Alfred often seems to be addressing a Welsh audience and makes many comments critical of the Anglo-Saxons (though not their king!). It is possible that the biography was composed in the context of the Welsh kings' alliance with Alfred,[21] perhaps to impress on them the desirability of being associated with such a superior ruler (though it has also been suggested that Asser wrote to justify his absence from ecclesiastical duties in Wales). Such a political context for the work may also explain why it was abandoned, apparently incomplete, and seems never to have been circulated. In 893, the very year in which Asser says he was writing his *Life*,[22] Alfred entered a new relationship with Anarawd of Gwynedd, who had previously been allied with the Viking King of York but now sought Alfred's overlordship on the same terms as Æthelred of Mercia. This was a good opportunity for Alfred to neutralise potential enemies at a time when he was having to deal with a new Viking force, but it may not have suited the interests of the southern Welsh kings who had suffered years of bullying from Anarawd and his brothers. Perhaps there was no longer a market in Wales for an encomium of Alfred – or perhaps it was no longer needed now that all the Welsh princes were on board.

Alfred was, in short, more than just a King of Wessex. This was reflected in the regnal titles applied to him. Asser dedicated his work to 'my esteemed and most holy lord, Alfred, ruler of all the Christians of the Island of Britain, King of the Angles and Saxons'. Note the distinction between Alfred's overlordship, which included the Welsh, and the areas which Alfred ruled directly as king. The former title, something of an exaggeration, recalls the reference to his grandfather as *bretwalda*, one of the possible meanings of which was 'ruler of Britain'. His regnal title reflects the fact that Alfred now claimed kingship of parts of Anglian Mercia as well as the Saxon south – these divisions into Saxon and Anglian areas go back to the sixth century. 'King of the Anglo-Saxons' was increasingly used as a title in the latter part of Alfred's reign to reflect this new reality. Alfred was also styled 'King of the English' rather than 'King of the Saxons'. In the treaty with Guthrum, for instance, he claims to represent the people of England, 'Angelcynn'. A preference for the term 'English' over 'Saxon' seems to have been emerging at this time in the Church, partly because Pope Gregory the Great, who had sent a mission to the Anglo-Saxons and so was seen as their apostle, used the term 'English'; it was also the preferred form of Bede (himself an Anglian) in his *Ecclesiastical History of the English People*. 'English' and 'England' also had the advantage of distinguishing the Anglo-Saxons from those of continental Saxony – one of the areas from which settlers had originally come to Britain in the fifth century. Whatever the reason, it was extremely helpful to Alfred's reputation in subsequent centuries when he was seen as the founder of England and of English literature. Neither of these claims was completely true, but Alfred undoubtedly *did* rule more of England than anyone else during his lifetime, and he *did* use works written in Old English to underpin his position.

One year that seems to have been particularly important in the history of Alfred's overlordship was 886. The *Chronicle* records: 'King Alfred occupied London; and all the English people (*Angelcynn*) that were not under subjection to the Danes submitted to him. And then he entrusted the borough to the control of Ealdorman Æthelred.'[23]

Asser records that Alfred 'restored' the city of London and made it habitable again.[24] This seems to be the point at which the Middle Saxon trading enclave of London, hitherto based in the Covent Garden and Strand area, was moved inside the Roman walled area with its church at St Paul's, the cathedral centre of the East Saxons. The city's fortifications were also refurbished at this time and new streets and wharves laid out (referred to in land grants from the latter part of Alfred's reign.) Tree-ring dates from large timbers used in river frontages in the city support the suggestion of a major redevelopment programme in 886.

Alfred also celebrated his achievements in London with a special coin spelling out the Latin name 'Londinium' on one side and with a fine portrait of himself on the other.

We can imagine major celebrations and entertainments in London that year. It is possible that 886 was also the year when Æthelred of Mercia married Æthelflaed and a new concord was achieved between Wessex and Mercia, with Æthelred being given special responsibility for the administration and defence of London which had for many years been an important Mercian centre. Perhaps it was also in this year that the boundaries were negotiated which formed the subject of the treaty between Alfred and Guthrum.[25] The same word 'Angelcynn' appears in both the treaty and the *Chronicle* entry to describe the wide range of people recognising Alfred's authority and protection. But we remain uncertain about the exact events leading up to the climax of 886. A *Chronicle* entry for 883 reports very briefly that 'the English were encamped against the enemy army at London'. This seems to imply that Alfred had temporarily lost control of the city and then regained it – in itself a cause for celebration, and one which Alfred reinforced by refashioning London so that it could continue more securely its role as the great trading centre of southern England as well as a memorable showcase for his position as the only Anglo-Saxon overlord and king to have outfaced the Vikings.

Alfred undoubtedly belongs among the great Anglo-Saxon overlords, but how does he rate in European terms? Wessex was but a tiny area compared to the huge kingdom of Charlemagne, who controlled much of western Europe. Even when it was subdivided after the death of his son and successor Louis, the individual kingdoms inherited by Charlemagne's grandsons – who included Alfred's step-grandfather Charles the Bald – were much larger than Wessex. Francia, especially the parts bordering the North Sea and Channel, was afflicted by the same Viking raiders who came to England. Co-operation and intelligence-sharing between western Francia and England therefore made sense, and helps to explain the marriages of Judith to Alfred's father and brother Æthelbald. Reports on the movement of armies within Francia in the *Anglo-Saxon Chronicle* for the 880s suggest that connections were being maintained and information exchanged.

The *Chronicle* also records political developments within the Frankish realms, especially the quick turnover of kings. By the 880s, after a series of mishaps, there was a distinct shortage of descendants of Charlemagne in the male line. Francia began to fray at the edges as regions which were more remote from the centres of power became self-governing. One of these was the county of Flanders (straddling parts of the Netherlands and present-day Belgium). Before the end of his reign. Alfred's youngest daughter Ælfthryth had married Count Baldwin II of Flanders, son of Alfred's stepmother Judith by her third marriage (see Family Tree). Thus began the export (especially noted in the reigns of Alfred's son Edward and eldest grandson Athelstan) of Anglo-Saxon princesses to the courts of continental houses whose blood was not as royal as it could have been. The pedigree of Wessex, as laid out in the *Anglo-Saxon Chronicle*, together with Alfred's success against the Vikings which had left him as the only viable Anglo-Saxon king, had undoubtedly raised the stock of Wessex on the continent in the course of his reign.

Alfred already had active connections with the continent, stretching back to his overseas travels as a young child, and it is likely he had kept up links with the religious houses established there by his father. Asser refers to the number of foreigners at Alfred's court; men from Francia were employed as craftsmen, warriors and churchmen.[26] Alfred was conscious that the English Church and culture lagged behind the sophisticated achievements of the Carolingian Renaissance initiated by Charlemagne. Frankish influences, including individual Frankish scholars, were to play an important part of Alfred's reforming agenda – and in his attempts to strengthen his country still further.

4

The Years of Reconstruction, 878–92 (2): Learning and Religion

Therefore it seems better to me – if it seems so to you – that we should turn into the language that we can all understand certain books which are necessary for all men to know.

King Alfred, c. 890[27]

Asser describes Alfred as 'ruler of all the Christians of Britain', and stresses religion as a major cultural difference between the English and Welsh on the one hand, and the Vikings on the other. Like other Anglo-Saxons, it would not have occurred to Alfred to doubt the existence of God, and he would also have believed that God could intervene to ensure victory for those who followed Him. Asser records Alfred's personal piety, his regular attendance at church, his praying and seeking the intervention of the saints. Alfred was especially devoted to Rome, the epicentre of Western Christianity, which he had visited as a child. He sent regular payments of alms to the Holy See. These were delivered by ealdormen and duly noted in the *Anglo-Saxon Chronicle*. In exchange a gift from Pope Marinus of a fragment of the Cross is recorded for 884, as is the fact that he freed from taxation the English 'school' in Rome founded by Alfred's forebear King Ine. Alfred also responded to a plea for funds from the Patriarch of Jerusalem in 881,[28] and in return received remedies from him for his abdominal problems.

Such personal piety and support for the wider Church would have been quite normal in this period. Alfred may also have been influenced by the potent example of

Charlemagne, who had vastly increased the area of Europe under Frankish rule, revived the title of Roman Emperor in the west and had also initiated the revival of religion, learning and the arts known to modern historians as the Carolingian Renaissance. Alfred had a number of personal links with Francia. How embarrassing for him, then, when he wished to correspond with his overseas contacts, that there was scarcely anyone in his kingdom who could write a decent letter in Latin, the language of learning, the Church and diplomacy throughout the period. Probably in around 890 Alfred wrote a letter to his bishops, which served as a preface to an English translation of Pope Gregory I's *Pastoral Care*, complaining about this lack and calling for an improvement.[29]

In the seventh and early eighth centuries during the conversion of the Anglo-Saxons to Christianity England had had notable schools and scholars who were as good as any in Europe. This was a golden age for scholarship, recorded for posterity through the works of Bede, its most eminent luminary. But in the ninth century there was a falling away. In his letter to the bishops, Alfred was inclined to blame the Vikings for the state of affairs. Their attacks on religious houses as easy sources of wealth did not help, but this was not the full explanation, especially for much of Wessex, where few of these types of attacks were recorded. A greater problem was that many religious houses had disappeared or been reclaimed by royal and noble families who then failed to provide adequate patronage and support. Alfred's will includes the estates of several former religious communities, which suggests where some of the family's new wealth under his grandfather Ecgbert had come from.[30] Alfred did found two major new religious houses during the course of his reign – a nunnery at Shaftesbury where his middle daughter served as abbess, and a monastery at Athelney to honour the place where he had survived his darkest hour.[31] But he was not nearly as generous to the Church as many other Anglo-Saxon kings, and relatively few charters from his time record grants of land to the Church. Asser, influenced by biblical accounts of Solomon, claims that Alfred devoted half his annual income to religious and charitable purposes,[32] but there is little sign of such generosity in Alfred's will. In fact, in contrast to many other lay bequests, the king left no land to the Church, only money for individual churchmen to whom he was particularly close and for care of his body and soul.

Moreover, Alfred seems to have retained much land that had once been used to support the Church. It is likely that his priority was spending on defensive measures. The Abbey of Abingdon remembered Alfred as a 'Judas' because he had used its land as a royal estate. Pope John VIII, in a letter to the Archbishop of Canterbury, refers to infringements of the latter's rights by the king.[33] Fulk, the Archbishop of Rheims, also expresses concerns about the quality of Christian life in Wessex, concerns later echoed by Asser.[34] There were still several significant religious houses in the kingdom, such as those at Malmesbury and Glastonbury, as well as bishoprics or archbishoprics at

Canterbury, Rochester, Selsey, Winchester and Sherborne; but the level of learning in them and knowledge of Latin seems to have been low. There were serious implications for standards of Christian knowledge and worship in the kingdom.

Alfred's determination to do something about this – but without denting too seriously the income that was needed for other purposes – coincided with the revival of his political fortune following the Battle of Edington, and was part of the same process. Overlordship of Mercia and southern Wales, both areas where educational provision seems to have been of higher quality, brought to Alfred's court in the mid-880s churchmen such as Waerferth, Bishop of Worcester, and Asser from St David's. These new arrivals, according to Asser, stimulated the king's interest in learning. Alfred had books read to him by the Mercians from the household of Waerferth, and Asser claims that he himself taught the king to read Latin.[35] Alfred also recruited two learned churchmen from the Frankish Empire: Grimbald of St Bertin (provided by Archbishop Fulk of Rheims) and John the Old Saxon (from German Saxony).

In bringing together these men of learning from different parts of Britain and Europe, Alfred imitated, perhaps intentionally, Charlemagne's recruitment of foreign scholars to spearhead a revival of Christian culture in Francia. The results in England were more modest, but still effective, though the texts produced were in English not Latin. This amount of translation into the native language was unusual, though not unprecedented: it may show the influence of Mercian traditions, or perhaps it shows the king's practical and pragmatic response. Many Anglo-Saxons were in the position that Alfred had been in until recently – able to read in their native language, but not in Latin. It therefore made sense to have more key works available in a language that everyone in England could understand.

The first work in this scheme was a commission from Alfred for Bishop Waerferth of Worcester to translate *The Dialogues* of Pope Gregory the Great. There followed a series of translations into Old English of key Latin texts, including the *Pastoral Care* of Gregory the Great, Boethius' *The Consolation of Philosophy*, the *Soliloquies* of St Augustine, the first fifty psalms and Orosius' *Histories against the Pagans*. Four of the works have prefaces attributing translation to Alfred himself, while the Orosius includes accounts of Scandinavia and the Baltic made by two travellers to Alfred's court.

Did Alfred, with all his other concerns and commitments, really translate these books in person? Could someone who had received very little education in his youth have mastered Latin so completely that he could render such major works into idiomatic English? Although the role of Alfred was accepted as fact for a long time, it is now regarded with greater scepticism. It was not an uncommon medieval practice to credit a patron with authorship of works that he had commissioned. Alfred's letter to his bishops which prefaces the translation of Gregory's *Pastoral Care* claims something rather less than the king's total authorship.[36] The bulk of the translation work is attributed to Asser, Grimbald and other scholars who, one might suspect, would then have expounded it to the king for final approval. Not only is such a method of working more realistic; it would help to explain the peculiarities of some of the texts, which occasionally depart from their originals in unexpected and sometimes unorthodox ways. The translation of Boethius, for instance, contains both a standard Christian rejection of pagan mythology and also an apparently contradictory impassioned defence of the great heroes of the past – with favourable mentions of the Germanic Weland and the classical hero-god Hercules. One can imagine Alfred, who according to Asser had been brought up on heroic literature, insisting on such an intervention to support something in which he believed strongly, even if it went against the spirit of the original text.

The *Pastoral Care* was the only one of the works to be widely circulated. The prefatory letter indicates that Alfred ordered a copy to be made and sent to each of his bishops. Pope Gregory had written the work as moral guidance for his own bishops and priests, and Alfred's letter makes it clear that he expects his bishops to act upon its example if they wish to keep his favour. He backed up his command in a very Anglo-Saxon way by including the gift of a valuable *aestel*, a decorative pointer designed to help the reader pick out the letters without damaging the text. The magnificent Alfred Jewel now on display in the Ashmolean Museum in Oxford may be representative of the *aestels* sent out on this occasion. By accepting such a gift the bishops would be under an even greater obligation to carry out Alfred's wishes. It also underlined one of the messages Alfred stresses in the letter – that wealth and wisdom come together; cultivate the latter, he argues, and the former (plus success in war) will follow. In this he pointed to the dream of King Solomon, who requested wisdom and understanding from God and received in addition riches and glory.[37] One can imagine how Alfred's scholarly advisers might have captured his attention with such allusions.

One of the qualities Alfred would have appreciated in his team's translations was their stress on the duty of loyal subjects as good Christians not only to obey God, but also the king as God's representative on earth. His new demands for building and garrisoning burhs had put extra burdens on the people of Wessex and had, according to Asser, met with some resistance.[38] It was the duty of the bishops to train the priests, who would then educate their parishioners in correct Christian behaviour – i.e. obedience.

Having issued these orders and sent copies of the *Pastoral Care*, Alfred seems to have left it to the bishops to take matters further. There is little sign that he instigated any major reorganisation of the Church. He did, however, support a school so that young men of free birth who showed ability could go on to be trained in Latin and become the next generation of priests 'as long as they are not useful for some other employment' (warfare, for example).[39] This school may have been based in one of the West Saxon religious houses, possibly Glastonbury, and Alfred's younger son Æthelweard seems to have received instruction in it. Alfred could also bolster his position by appointing men with the right ideas to bishoprics as they became vacant. In 890 Plegmund, one of the Mercian members of the translation team, was appointed Archbishop of Canterbury, and by the end of Alfred's reign Asser had been made Bishop of Sherborne. Alfred had done enough to turn the tide of decline in the Church, and tenth-century ecclesiastical reformers later acknowledged their debt to what had begun in his reign.

The *Pastoral Care* was deemed to provide guidance not only for churchmen, but for anyone in a position of authority, including kings. Collectively, the translations present an ideal of royal behaviour based on biblical texts and commentaries, leavened with Carolingian and Anglo-Saxon practicalities. Their tone permeates and influences much of the written evidence for Alfred and his reign. Alfred's laws, for instance, were prefaced with a long introduction linking them with Old Testament traditions of law-giving. Moreover, the ideals of the scholarly circle crucially informed how Asser portrayed the king in his biography, with the result that it is now difficult to separate ideal from reality.

The translation into Old English also subtly shifted the meaning of the texts so that they came closer to those of the poetic heroic world to whose standards Alfred would also have aspired. For instance, Old English *craeft* lacked the moral and specifically Christian connotations of the Latin word *virtus*. In the Old English translation of Boethius two non-Christian heroes, Weland and Hercules, are said to have displayed *craeft* when they brutally despatched their enemies. Weland, a talented smith, had, according to legend, been captured by an enemy king and lamed so that he could not escape. His revenge involved killing the king's sons, making cups from their skulls and raping their sister, whereupon he made his escape in some sort of flying-suit fashioned from bird feathers. The Old English version of Boethius, perhaps reflecting Alfred's own opinion, praises Weland for his wisdom, another key word in Alfredian texts, as well as his 'craft' – not just as a skilled smith, but as someone with the mental agility to get himself out of a difficult situation, qualities also shared with the great warrior hero Hercules in his battles with monsters. Acquisition of wealth and reputation are also praised in the Old English Boethius, rather against the spirit of the original, but instead reflecting heroic ideals to which the king may well have aspired. A lay reader such as Alfred might not have taken quite the lessons from these classic texts that his more scholarly advisers had hoped he would.

So, how far did Alfred himself subscribe to the ideals of kingship produced by his scholarly advisers, and how far did he attempt to live by them? This is an impossible question to answer conclusively. Asser suggests that Alfred was genuinely stimulated by his studies. As well as providing intellectual interest, they may have helped him to analyse situations, to appreciate more fully his moral responsibilities as king and to reconcile himself to sacrifices he had to make. With all the enthusiasm of the mature student, he seems to have felt that the laymen who held office under him, the ealdormen and reeves who supervised royal estates, would benefit from the same types of study that he had made. According to Asser, he insisted that they all read and studied, on pain of losing their positions, and many of them found it very difficult.[40] Alfred was said to be particularly concerned that those who acted as judges should apply themselves, for in the Anglo-Saxon way of doing things much depended on the probity of the individual and their capacity to make clear and objective moral judgements.

The different policies Alfred pursued after his victory at Edington in 878 were all part of a whole. Military rearmament was matched by religious reinforcement to ensure God's support, restore morale and encourage the king's subjects to follow his example. Alliances with other rulers in Britain increased the military force at Alfred's disposal. Patronage of churchmen helped him achieve a revival of learning in Wessex. Patronage of foreigners gave Alfred 'cultural capital', a more sophisticated and cosmopolitan feel to his court which was commensurate with his position as overlord. In all these various ways Alfred's position was greatly strengthened when he had to face a further series of serious Viking attacks towards the end of his reign.

5

The Last Battles, 892–99

893. And then King Alfred collected his army, and advanced to take up a position between the two enemy forces ... The king had divided his army into two, so that always half of it men were at home, half on service, apart from the men who guarded the boroughs.

Anglo-Saxon Chronicle

In 892 the event Alfred had been preparing for finally occurred. In that year a Viking army which had been campaigning for many years in Francia crossed the Channel and established a base at Appledore on Romney Marsh. It was soon joined by a second fleet under the veteran commander Hastein, who made a separate camp at Sittingbourne in north Kent. These armies meant business. They had come in around 350 ships, together with women, children and horses. Like the Great Army before them, they were not just in search of booty. They planned to seize land and settle. Some of them had probably taken part in the major raid on Kent seven years earlier, when Alfred had successfully besieged them in Rochester.

At first the West Saxon defences looked vulnerable. Alfred's new arrangements were not fully in place or working as well as they should have been. The main Viking fleet had been able to establish itself because a burh which could have halted it had not been completed and was unmanned. An attempt to win over Hastein with the type of ceremony and gift-giving that had worked with Guthrum failed. Alfred and Ealdorman Æthelred of Mercia both stood as godfather to one of the sons of Hastein in a baptismal ceremony underpinned by generous gifts. Hastein did agree to withdraw from his Kent base – but only to establish a new one at Benfleet on the north bank of the Thames in Essex.

Alfred's elder son Edward had to watch the bulk of his forces withdrawing from a siege because their period of service was up and their provisions consumed before replacements had arrived. (So much for Saxon plans to keep an army on permanent alert by having half the available forces on duty at any one time, while the other half rested at home.) There was also the major threat that Vikings already settled in eastern England would join up with the newcomers. Alfred had tried to persuade the Danes in East Anglia and Northumbria not to do this, but after the death in 890 of his ally Guthrum, his influence in eastern England was reduced. In 893 the East Anglian Vikings felt they had more to gain by attacking Wessex and sent fleets to north and south Devon. Alfred had to go with his part of the army to deal with them, leaving Ealdorman Æthelred and Prince Edward to deal with the incomers in the east.

Then the reforms made by Alfred began to pay off, and the West Saxons and their allies gradually gained the upper hand. What happened is described in new annals of the *Anglo-Saxon Chronicle*, which seem to have been compiled soon after the events they describe. They are much more detailed than those covering the campaigns of the 870s and so help us to understand more of the detailed manoeuvrings of both sides – though they are not always easy to follow, as the war was being fought across two widely spread fronts.

Crucial to Saxon success were the close links forged between Alfred and Ealdorman Æthelred of Mercia. Æthelred was a seasoned military commander, and the support of his Mercian forces, reinforced by a West Saxon contingent led by the inexperienced Prince Edward, meant that the Anglo-Saxons could field two major armies at any one time. There was also the potential for smaller units to be split off under the command of individual ealdormen, and for greater forces to be raised when necessary by calling out men from the burhs. One of the hallmarks of the Anglo-Saxon response in the 890s was its versatile ability to respond swiftly to changing circumstances. The strategy was to keep the Vikings on the move, never allowing them to establish permanent bases in West Saxon or Mercian territory, thereby preventing them from acquiring any fresh food or fodder. This policy of attrition, rather than engagement in direct battle, was to win the day.

While Alfred was occupied in Devon in 893, the Anglo-Saxon forces in the east stormed Hastein's base at Benfleet. The enemy took to their ships and 'went up along the Thames until they reached the Severn'. At Buttington, near Welshpool in Powys, they were besieged by a large army commanded by Æthelred, supplemented by forces called out from West Saxon and Mercian burhs and some Welsh allies. The encircled Vikings were forced to eat their horses and, when supplies finally ran out, they had no choice but to try to break the siege. They suffered a heavy defeat. Those few who managed to escape eventually made their way back to their safe haven in Essex, where they were joined by supporters from East Anglia and Northumbria.

The renewed Viking force then made its way to Chester. Once again, Æthelred's forces kept them contained and prevented them renewing supplies. Although the Vikings did eventually escape, they had not been able to establish themselves within Mercia. The enemy contingent in Exeter was similarly penned in by Alfred and eventually forced to withdraw. When they attempted to raid near Chichester on their way back to Essex, the local garrison came out from the burh and saw them off.

The year 895 opened with what was left of the enemy army holed up in a fortress on the river Lea about 20 miles north of London, near Hertford. Alfred continued the policy of making it impossible for them to get out and to renew their supplies. His forces stood guard over the fields so that the crops could be harvested to keep the garrison in London supplied. He also – probably in reaction to the events at Benfleet when the enemy had been able to escape upriver – built fortifications on both sides of the river further upstream so that that exit by boat was denied. Such double-burhs on rivers had been used successfully by the Franks. The Viking forces did manage to escape overland into Mercia, and shut themselves in Bridgnorth on the Welsh border for the winter, but it must have become evident to them that they were making no headway in securing new lands. The determined resistance of Alfred and Æthelred was proving highly effective. In 896, four years after they had first embarked on their assault, the Vikings finally gave up, and either went back to the continent or joined the existing settlers in eastern England.

Later that year Alfred experimented with building new, larger warships to deal with any future Viking threats. The *Anglo-Saxon Chronicle* describes these mighty vessels:

> They were almost twice as long as the others. Some had 60 oars, some more. They were both swifter and steadier and also higher than the others. They were built neither on the Frisian or Danish pattern, but as it seemed to him himself that they could be most useful.[41]

This is a good example of Alfred's inventiveness and attention to detail.

Alfred also continued to pursue diplomatic solutions. Some sort of alliance was formed around this time with the Viking kings Guthfrith and Sigeferth of York (the precise details are unclear).

Battle with the Vikings had dominated the entries in the *Anglo-Saxon Chronicle* between 892 and 896, so it comes of something of a surprise to read the laconic judgement at their conclusion that 'by the grace of God, the army had not on the whole afflicted the English people very greatly'. Far more serious, the chronicler writes, were plagues which took the lives of many men and cattle, and caused the loss of major noblemen in royal service. This is a reminder that the *Anglo-Saxon Chronicle* is a very selective account of events in Alfred reign and tells us little of domestic affairs in Wessex. It may give a misleading impression of apparent harmony in the kingdom. In Alfred's will there are hints of discord, with opposition to some of Alfred's military demands and his plans for the succession, while in Asser's biography there is a reference to Alfred having to punish opponents.[42]

The *Chronicle* records no events involving the king for the last three years of his life. That does not mean that nothing of significance happened, but if it did we know nothing about it. Although Asser outlived Alfred he apparently ceased writing in 893 and does not describe Alfred's last years. We do not know if Alfred had any particular intimations of mortality, but it would seem that plans for the succession had been in place for over a decade.[43] Alfred's will bequeathed large gifts of land to his elder son Edward, making it clear that he was to be Alfred's main heir and successor upon his death. Alfred further enhanced his son's position by giving Edward a major command during the Viking wars of the 890s, and may even have made him a junior king based in Kent shortly before his death. By contrast, the modest legacy to Alfred's second son Æthelweard and his lack of a public profile may suggest that he was very much a 'spare' – to be kept in reserve should anything happen to Edward. Alfred, it seems, hoped for what did indeed occur, namely, the establishment of a line of kings through Edward. Shortly before his death, Alfred presided at a formal ceremony to recognise his grandson Athelstan (the son of Edward) as eventual heir to the throne.[44] Athelstan was only about 4 or 5 when the ceremony took place – about the same age that Alfred had been when he made his first journey to Rome and received what he believed to be papal confirmation of his right to succeed as King of Wessex. Alfred seems to have tried to arrange something comparable for his grandson. He understood the importance of stability and wanted to guarantee the continuity of his royal lineage.

Matters were not so simple. Alfred could arrange for inherited royal estates to pass to a nominated heir, but only the chief lay and ecclesiastical nobles, known collectively as the witan, could decide who should be king, and Alfred's heirs were not the only candidates. Their chief rivals were Alfred's nephews, the sons of his predecessor, his older brother, Æthelred.

As Alfred explains in his will, he and Æthelred had made a risky pact.[45] When Æthelred succeeded to the throne in 865 he felt that he needed control and income from all the family estates in which he and Alfred had a joint interest. Alfred agreed to this, but on condition that the heirs of whichever of the two of them lived the longest would succeed to everything, leaving only a small number of estates for those dispossessed. In other words, in agreeing to this arrangement, Æthelred authorised the dispossession of his own sons should he die before Alfred – and that is exactly what happened. In Alfred's will his nephews get only the small number of estates agreed with

Æthelred. They had little discernible public role during Alfred's reign and are not referred to by Asser or in the *Anglo-Saxon Chronicle*. It seems clear that Alfred did not want them to have any rights to the throne.

We should note that it is only Alfred's version of events which survives. In his will he admits that the nephews were not happy with the situation and that they had their supporters. This may help to explain an apparent dip in support for Alfred immediately after Æthelred's death in 871 in spite of the serious situation with the Vikings. Alfred refers in the will to a challenge to his interpretation of the arrangements, perhaps made soon after his accession, but that his view was upheld by the witan and he prevailed.

That at least one of the nephews, Æthelwold, believed he had been unjustly barred from the succession is suggested by his attempt to take the throne immediately after Alfred's death. Although Æthelwold apparently won little support in Wessex, he posed a real danger to Edward because when he left Wessex he sought out the Vikings in Northumbria, who recognised him as king. With Viking help Æthelwold put together a fleet, and in 901 established himself in Essex, from where he raided into Wiltshire. His bid for the throne was ended in 902 when he was defeated and killed in battle with Edward at Holme (Essex), but he clearly posed a real threat to Alfred's plans for the succession. It is likely that had his nephews left an account of their Uncle Alfred's reign he would have appeared in a rather different light from that constructed for him by Asser.

We know that Alfred died on 26 October 899, but that is all we know. We do not know how or why he died then, or where. He would have been about 50, which seems relatively young today and we might be inclined to blame his death on his mystery illness. But 50 would not be considered abnormally young at the time, especially when we consider that Alfred spent long periods on campaign in all weathers. Quite minor problems and injuries that can be treated readily with antibiotics today could easily become fatal in the early Middle Ages. Alfred's son Edward died at about the same age, and his grandson Athelstan in his early 40s. Alfred was buried in the Old Minster, the cathedral church of Winchester, the premier West Saxon bishopric and burial place of several West Saxon kings, including his father and grandfather. Soon afterwards, his son Edward ordered the building of a grand new church in the contemporary Frankish style right next to the Old Minster, imaginatively known as the New Minster. Although only parts of its plan are known, the new church seems to have had close parallels with St Denis near Paris, which Charlemagne had rebuilt for the burial of his father Pepin. Perhaps Edward was deliberately drawing parallels between himself, his father and these great Frankish kings – to assert that Alfred had in effect founded a new royal line as King of the Anglo-Saxons, and that only his heirs should rule in future. (His cousin Æthelwold had attempted a coup and was still at large when work began on New Minster.) A few years later Alfred's body was moved there, together with that of his wife Ealhswith, who died in 902, and his Frankish adviser Grimbald, who died in 901 having spent his last years in Winchester. Subsequently Edward, his brother and one of his sons would also be buried there.

In 1110 Alfred's body was transferred again when New Minster moved out of the crowded town centre to a more spacious site in the northern suburb of Hyde. His and Edward's graves may have survived the dissolution of Hyde Abbey in 1538, but they were unceremoniously turned out when the land was developed at the end of the eighteenth century. What was possibly a piece of the king's pelvis was identified by radio-carbon dating in 2014 (though it is equally likely to be Edward's, since he was buried next to Alfred in Hyde Abbey). Just possibly more of his body may eventually be recovered and, if we are very lucky, it could throw light on the problems of the king's health and the cause of his death as well as establishing a sense of his build and general appearance.

The *Anglo-Saxon Chronicle* is very matter-of-fact in its account of Alfred's death, and records as his greatest achievement that 'he was king over the whole English people, except for that part which was under Danish rule'. Perhaps surprisingly the greatest recorded Anglo-Saxon tribute to Alfred comes from a descendant of one of his nephews. This was Æthelweard, ealdorman of the western shires, who at the end of the tenth century produced – or had produced for him – a Latin translation of the *Chronicle* (a significant source as it contains additional material not in the surviving Old English versions). Æthelweard's interest in his family's history and the written word is in itself a tribute to Alfred's campaign to raise standards of learning among the nobility. His epitaph for his kinsman suggests the importance of Alfred's personal example:

> Magnanimous Alfred passed from the world, king of the Saxons, unshakeable pillar of the western people, a man replete with justice, vigorous in warfare, learned in speech, above all instructed in divine learning. For he had translated unknown numbers of books from rhetorical Latin speech into his own language.[46]

In the centuries following his death the achievements attributed to Alfred were destined to grow and grow.

6

Alfred's Posthumous Reputation

Alfred found learning dead, and he restored it. Education neglected, and he revived it. The laws powerless, and he gave them force. The Church debased, and he raised it. The land ravaged by a fearful enemy, from which he delivered it. Alfred's name will live as long as mankind shall respect the past.

Inscription on King Alfred's statue at Wantage

Most biographical studies end with the death of their subject – but in Alfred's case the spectacular growth of his posthumous reputation is an essential part of his story. The designation of Alfred as 'the Great' was made a considerable time after his death (in contrast to that of the medieval Frankish ruler Charlemagne, 'Carolus Magnus', who was recognised as a giant even in his own lifetime). It was first bestowed by Matthew Paris, a thirteenth-century chronicler from St Albans, but did not receive wide currency until the sixteenth century. It was then that Alfred's reputation really took off. Alfred became, in effect, the icon for all things positive about the Anglo-Saxon period and was credited with the achievements of all the kings from 400 to 1066. As the best-known representative of the Anglo-Saxon past, many anachronisms from later periods were projected onto him. The result is that there is still much popular confusion about what Alfred did actually achieve and what he may really have been like. Any assessment of his reputation must, therefore, strip away these accretions through an understanding of how and why they occurred.

Alfred was not perceived as the founder of his dynasty's greatness in the way that Charlemagne was among the

Franks. His son Edward (r. 899–924) and grandson Athelstan (r. 924–39) both made major conquests of the Viking-held areas of England and so ruled larger territories than Alfred had done. Athelstan was the first to rule the entirety of England and after a great victory at the Battle of Brunaburh in 937 he was recognised by all the other rulers of Britain as their overlord. But neither Edward nor Athelstan left behind the range of sources which has been so important for Alfred's reputation – the written works and also the oral traditions centred on the period of Alfred's retreat to Athelney after Guthrum's invasion of Wessex in 878. The latter have come down to us through literature associated with St Neot and St Cuthbert and via the twelfth-century historian William of Malmesbury in his *History of the English Kings*. The cake-burning story, for example, which has become so closely linked with Alfred, ironically derives from various works celebrating St Neot (who, completely implausibly, is claimed as Alfred's brother.)[47] Neot is the hero of these stories rather than his unsatisfactory 'brother' Alfred, who is said to have brought troubles on himself as God's judgement for previous bad behaviour. Neot's teaching eventually helps Alfred achieve a Job-like stoicism, and the saint then intervenes on behalf of a repentant king.

Alfred would surely have preferred the story preserved by the twelfth-century historian William of Malmesbury, in which he was the agent of his own success. This version recounts how he left the stronghold of Athelney in order to infiltrate Guthrum's camp disguised as a minstrel.

After staying there several days without detection Alfred was able to discover the enemy's battle-plans and so defeat Guthrum at the Battle of Edington[48] Superficially this may sound a plausible account of Alfred, combining his love of traditional Old English verse with the type of cunning stratagem one might expect from a successful early medieval warrior. Sadly, it seems to be one of the floating stories of the Middle Ages which became attached to more than one monarch. William himself only a few pages later describes a Viking leader called Anlaf using the same minstrel-disguise ploy on Alfred's grandson Athelstan.[49] Alfred as minstrel is as unlikely as Alfred as Neot's brother.

Alfred's promotion of books and learning, which for some later Anglo-Saxon writers marked him out from other kings, also had a more popular manifestation. Various traditional sayings are attributed to him in Middle English texts of the thirteenth century. But what was ultimately most important for the growth of his reputation was the relatively large amount of written material that survived from his reign, especially his law code, the *Anglo-Saxon Chronicle* and, above all, the biography written by Asser.

The growth of Alfred's reputation began in the Middle Ages. Chroniclers started nudging his achievements just a bit further than was actually warranted – until quite far-fetched claims were being made in his name. By the end of the Middle Ages Alfred had become not only king of all England, but also the founder of the entire

Anglo-Saxon system of local government, the shires and their subdivisions (actually the result of much longer, complex developments).

In the middle of the fourteenth century Alfred was claimed as the founder of University College, Oxford, through an imaginative promotion of his recruitment of scholars and foundation of a court school. In the following century Grimbald had been recast as Oxford's first Professor of Divinity, while Asser was given charge of instruction in grammar and rhetoric. Oxford's claims persisted well into the nineteenth century and received bogus support through the insertion of a passage about these spurious origins into a printed edition of Asser's biography in 1602.

It was in the Reformation that Alfred's reputation really began to take off. The Elizabethan Archbishop of Canterbury, Matthew Parker (in office 1559–75), collected and published many key Alfredian texts, thus saving them from destruction after the dissolution of the monastic libraries in which they had been housed. He found them particularly useful for supporting his claim that the Anglican Church constituted not so much a rejection of Roman Catholic traditions as a return to the practices of the Anglo-Saxon period. Like most quests for Anglo-Saxon origins, this represented wish-fulfilment rather than what had actually been the case: Alfred's reconfiguration as an English Protestant hero required ignoring the fact that he had strong links to Rome and to the cult of saints.

In the internecine strife of the seventeenth century, the Anglo-Saxon past was also evoked by those hoping for more parliamentary and civil liberties. These were similarly presented as a return to Anglo-Saxon freedoms which had been lost after the Norman Conquest. As many campaigners wanted to limit rather than boost royal power, Alfred was not such a hero to them, though his law code was used to support claims for parliamentary origins in the Anglo-Saxon witan. A late medieval tradition that Alfred had forty-four judges hanged for giving unjust judgements also gave him a favourable reception among later would-be law reformers. The stage was set for Alfred to achieve greatness as the founder of the English constitution and all other manifestations of English identity in the following century.

The accession of the Hanoverian dynasty, who were dukes of continental Saxony, opened up the possibility of making various political points by drawing parallels or contrasts with their Anglo-Saxon forebears. The most striking manifestation was created by those Whigs and disaffected Tories opposed to the policies of George II's chief minister, Robert Walpole. They accused him of suppressing parliamentary freedoms, failure to support the naval war against Spain, and corruption. George II was tainted by association, and the criticisms of him were intensified by comparing him with a true 'patriot' king, namely Alfred. One of the leaders of the anti-Walpole faction was Lord Cobham, who used his pleasure gardens at Stowe in Buckinghamshire to contrast modern sleaze with Saxon probity. A bust of Alfred was erected in the 'Temple of British Worthies' (which can still be seen) with the following inscription: 'The mildest, justest, most beneficent of kings who drove out the Danes, secured the seas, protected learning, established juries, crushed corruption, guarded liberty and was the founder of the English constitution.' Alfred could not claim to be the founder of juries, and he would have been very surprised to be promoted as a protector of parliamentary liberties, of which he would have had no experience. This is an Alfred reimagined in a very specific eighteenth-century political context.

From this point on, Alfred began to impinge more comprehensively on popular consciousness. 'Rule Britannia' began life as an anthem written by Thomas Arne for a royal masque about Alfred. It became a popular patriotic song during the Napoleonic wars, and Alfred rose with it as a symbol of earlier naval successes against foreign invasion. He became the subject of plays, poems, paintings and engravings as well as popular histories. There was even an Alfred pantomime in which Alfred and two of his men blacked up and went to Guthrum's camp disguised as black minstrels.

Wealthy or influential patrons imposed reminiscences of Alfred on to the landscape. Henry Hoare erected the 160ft King Alfred's Tower on his estate at Stourhead, Wiltshire, in 1772 in the place where he claimed the king had assembled his army before the Battle of Edington. Other battles had occurred on the Berkshire Downs near

Alfred's birthplace at Wantage. A series of prehistoric monuments in the area became associated with the king's campaigns. The prehistoric long barrow of Wayland's Smithy was identified as the burial place of defeated Viking leaders, the late Bronze Age White Horse of Uffington was said to have been carved on the orders of Alfred to celebrate his victory at the Battle of Ashdown, and a nearby Iron Age hillfort was dubbed Alfred's Castle.

The climax of the Berkshire appropriations of Alfred's memory was the unveiling of his statue in Wantage by Prince Edward (later Edward VII) and Princess Alexandra in 1877. The sculptor, Count Gleichen, was a relative of Prince Albert, and the statue had been paid for by the local MP and landowner Robert Lloyd-Lindsay (later Lord Wantage), a former equerry to the Prince of Wales. Alfred had been claimed by the Establishment as one of its own.

By this stage in Queen Victoria's reign Alfred had come to be seen not only as the founder of much of the English constitution but also as a representative of all that was best in the Anglo-Saxon English character. As what was known of Alfred's personality came through the idealising works of his court circle – in which he was depicted as moral, pious, brave and intelligent – such a precedent was extremely flattering to Victorian sensibilities. It seemed to reflect back to them their ideals of the perfect Englishman – perhaps even, as the historian Edward Freeman claimed, 'the most perfect character in history'.[50]

Alfred's apparent desire to improve the lives of his subjects also fitted well with ideas of Victorian philanthropy at home and abroad. Parallels were drawn between his conversion of Guthrum's followers and the work of Christian missionaries in the British colonies. Imperial expansion could be portrayed as an opportunity to export Alfred's constitution to parts of the globe which had not had the advantage of Anglo-Saxon origins.

It was this desire to celebrate the Anglo-Saxon origins of the British Empire that lay behind the most impressive Alfredian commemoration of all, on the millenary of his death in 1901. The events took place during the Boer War, when an opportunity for rousing patriotism seemed particularly desirable. The climax of three days of celebrations was the unveiling of the huge bronze statue by Hamo Thornycroft which stands to this day in Winchester, the place of Alfred's burial. Thornycroft described his monument as 'two and a half times as high as nature and therefore about fourteen times as big as life'.[51] Manoeuvring the statue, and the two large granite monoliths on which it stands, through the streets of Winchester, and then erecting them at the east end of the town, were epic events in themselves – and possibly the most exciting thing to have happened in Winchester since it was stormed by Vikings in 860. Alfred holds his sword aloft so that the hilt and blade form the sign of the Cross, a symbolism that was much appreciated at the time and seen to embody the concept that Alfred's battles were fought to protect England as a Christian nation.[52]

The statue was unveiled by the former prime minister, Lord Rosebery; mourning etiquette following the recent death of Queen Victoria prevented any royal from doing so. Rosebery had no qualms in yoking the achievements of Alfred with the creation of the British Empire. Nor did he shy away from awareness that the past was being manipulated to support the needs of the present:

> How is it that we have now gone back a thousand years to find a great hero with whom we may associate something of English grandeur, and the origin of much that makes England powerful? Is it not the growing sense of British empire, the increased feeling, not for bastard, but for real Imperialism? With a present not always cheerful, with a remote past so small and yet so pregnant, we yet dignify and sanctify our own aspirations by referring them to the historic past.[53]

The ceremony took place in front of representatives from all ranks of the British political and ecclesiastical establishment and from distinguished centres of learning throughout the British Empire and America – Americans who claimed English origins also embraced Alfred as a fitting forebear. 'He was our king just as much as yours,' said the leading American delegate replying to the toast 'The Anglo-Saxon Race, and the Memory of Alfred' at the mayoral luncheon. He celebrated the characteristics which Americans and English shared from their Anglo-Saxon past and which made them, together, 'the dominant race of the world'.[54] The ceremony reinforced the common interests of British imperialists and the strong 'Anglo-Saxonist' element in the American government.

The millenary was the occasion that produced some of the most exaggerated claims for Alfredian precedents. Alfred was said, for instance, to have anticipated Victorian provision of universal education: 'his standard was that every boy and girl in the whole of the nation should be able to read and write,' claimed Arthur Conan Doyle.[55] This, of course, was a gross distortion of Alfred's much more limited plans and his provision of a solitary court school. He may have given his son Edward and his youngest daughter a similar education, but he certainly had not concerned himself with the education of anybody else's daughters.

Claims that Alfred was the founder of the English navy, which spawned a succession of HMS *King Alfred*s, also exaggerate a grain of truth. Alfred did involve himself in the design of new ships in 896, but he did not create 'a navy' where none had existed before. The Anglo-Saxons were a North Sea people and had always used ships to aid warfare when appropriate. Alfred's brothers, father and grandfather had all successfully deployed ships against the Vikings. Attribution to Alfred was a shorthand way of claiming Anglo-Saxon antiquity for relatively new Victorian institutions, organised on a different scale and with different aims from those of their distant antecedents.

Any reputation that Alfred has today is but a pale shadow of the outpourings of 1901. In the long run, yoking his reputation to the destiny of the British Empire may have done him more harm than good. Attempts to invoke his support for English superiority over other peoples feels embarrassingly inappropriate today. Alfred's Christian identity has also reduced his current appeal: the amoral, internationally-minded Vikings seem to be the early medieval people of choice today.

There are, however, many pockets of interest in Alfred which have endured, unshackled from attempts to make him a symbol for developments of which he can never have had any inkling. There are places still proud to register an association with the king. Pewsey, which had an Alfred statue erected in 1913 and was a former royal estate, still celebrates him with an annual carnival. Winchester's statue of Alfred is frequently chosen as Winchester's icon in a weekly poll in the *Hampshire Chronicle*. The inhabitants of the Winchester suburb of Hyde, which was Alfred's last known burial place, led the campaign for a major archaeological search for his remains. Subsequent coverage by the national press showed that Alfred's name was still big enough to command wide interest and attention. But are we in any better position than our Victorian predecessors to recognise the 'real' King Alfred?

7

Conclusion: Alfred's Character and Achievements

Meanwhile the king, amidst the wars and the numerous interruptions of this present life … did not refrain from directing the government of the kingdom; pursuing all manner of hunting; giving instruction to all his goldsmiths and craftsmen as well as to his falconers, hawk-trainers and dog-keepers; making to his own design wonderful and precious new treasures.

Asser, 893[56]

Drawing conclusions about any character from history – especially one who died over a thousand years ago – is fraught with difficulties. There are so many aspects of the medieval mind that are obscure for us today. In Alfred's case we have a relatively clear idea of how the men of learning at his court wanted him to be portrayed for posterity: as a model of Christian kingship. Alfred may well have approved of many aspects of this model and aspired to live up to their ideals, but if we do not wish to subscribe to Victorian hagiography we have to dig deeper to try to uncover something of the reality behind the idealised portrait.

One approach is to look for contemporary assessments of Alfred which were not those of the court scholars. There is a limited amount of such information, but enough to provide insights which can then be related to aspects recorded in the better-known sources.

One such insight comes in a memorandum from the reign of Alfred's son Edward. It is known as the Fonthill letter and concerns a complicated set of legal proceedings over the disputed ownership of the eponymous Wiltshire estate.[57] The narrator of the memorandum is Ordlaf, who had been appointed ealdorman of Wiltshire towards the end of Alfred's reign. At one point Ordlaf exclaims, 'If one wishes to alter every judgement that King Alfred made, when shall we then have finished disputing?' The implication is that Alfred intervened in a large number of such disputes, which fits with what Asser says about Alfred being very concerned with legal matters.[58] The Fonthill letter also provides an interesting cameo of Alfred making a legal judgement. We read of various aggrieved parties, including Ordlaf, presenting an aspect of the dispute to the king while he is washing his hands in his private chamber at nearby Wardour. Royal judgements, it seems, could be made in such informal settings and did not have to involve a court of law.

The document further reveals the difficulties Alfred would have had in making any major changes to the legal system, for settlements were based upon the traditional practice of oath-swearing, valued in accordance with social status, and the use of monetary payment from one party to the other; the king could usually expect to receive some proportion of the claim when royal justice was invoked.

The challenge to ownership of the Fonthill estate had arisen because a nobleman called Helmstan had stolen another's belt – this could be an expensive item with many silver or gilt fittings. He had been found guilty and so his oath had lost its value and he could not use it to defend his ownership of the estate. But Helmstan had influential connections, including Ealdorman Ordlaf, who was his godfather, and it was Ordlaf who persuaded the king to give him a second chance – though, as subsequent events showed, Helmstan was a persistent malefactor who was eventually had up for cattle-rustling. Alfred was therefore very much part of a tradition where wealth, status and having the right connections helped to sway judgements in an individual's favour. With Viking attacks always in the offing, he was in no position to bring about major structural changes to the entire legal system.

For all its grandiose preface, Alfred's law code is deeply traditional. There is little evidence of a major attempt to link its main contents with a stronger Christian morality as seen, for example, in Frankish legislation. It is presented as supplementing the law code of his predecessor King Ine. Some of the laws recorded in it seem to be original judgements designed to suit unusual circumstances and arguably represent verdicts handed down by Alfred himself. One provision, for instance, defines who is at fault if someone manages to transfix himself upon a spear carried over the shoulder of another – perhaps a problem that arose in military manoeuvres. The perils of Anglo-Saxon woodland management emerge in a further example:

> If one man kills another unintentionally [by allowing a tree to fall on him] while they are engaged on a common task, the tree shall be given to the [dead man's kindred], and they shall remove it within 30 days from the locality. Otherwise, it shall be taken by him who owns the wood.[59]

The precision of the judgment is intriguing. Surely a real case must lie behind such a clause? Ordlaf's comment on Alfred in the Fonthill letter suggests that the king was interventionist and kept a close eye on what his officials were doing in his name. This is confirmed by Asser, who refers to Alfred not only concerning himself with details of government, but 'giving instruction to all his goldsmiths and craftsmen as well as to his falconers, hawk-trainers and dog-keepers ... issuing orders to all his followers; all these things he did himself with great application to the best of his abilities.'[60] Here we may have an important key to Alfred's character and to the success of his reign. It seems he was, in modern parlance, a micromanager, a man who left nothing to chance and checked that his orders were being obeyed, even down to the duties of those in charge of his hunting dogs.

Asser brings out this aspect of Alfred's character in relation to the building of fortresses.[61] There was clearly some resistance to royal orders from men who feared it would involve too much time, effort and expense. Alfred therefore kept a close eye on what was or was not being done, and, 'by gently instructing, cajoling, urging commanding and (in the end when his patience was exhausted) by sharply chastising', got the work completed. As Ordlaf seems to acknowledge, Alfred kept people on their toes and in this way, it seems, he gained results.

The building of the burhs also fits with another Alfredian character trait: his inventiveness. The *Anglo-Saxon Chronicle* entry for 896 records how the king commissioned new ships and took a personal interest in ensuring the models which 'as it seemed to him himself ... could be most useful'. Asser gives another example in his description of the king's invention of a candle clock:

> He instructed his chaplains to produce an ample quantity of wax, and when they had brought it, he told them to weigh it against the weight of pennies on a two-pound balance. When a sufficient amount of wax, equivalent in weight to seventy-two pennies, had been measured out, he told the chaplains to make six candles out of it, each of equal size, so that each candle would be twelve inches long and would have the inches marked on it... the six candles could burn one after the other without interruption through the course of the twenty-four hours.[62]

Draughty royal residences and tents meant the candles kept guttering – whereupon the king devised nifty lanterns of wood and ox-horn to protect them. Here we seem to see not only Alfred's ingenuity, but also perhaps a certain obsession with apportioning his time exactly (though Asser links this with a desire to keep regular devotional hours).

This inventiveness goes hand-in-hand with the intellectual curiosity attributed to the king by Asser, and which also seems to be supported by Alfred's concern to commission the translation of key Latin works into Old English – an endeavour with which, typically it would seem, he also involved himself directly. One forms the impression that the king realised the power of literature to sharpen his mind and wanted others in his service to improve themselves similarly. He may indeed have received direct inspiration from the translated works. The Old English translation of Orosius describes the Amazonian army as divided 'into two parts, one of which remained at home to guard their land, the other of which went out on campaign to wage war'.[63] The *Anglo-Saxon Chronicle*'s description of Alfred's division of his army in 893 is couched in very similar terms, raising the intriguing possibility that Alfred may have honed his tactics in the light of what he read.

The Orosius translation also contains some new geographical material on northern Europe which appears to have been inserted at Alfred's behest. Reports in it of Alfred's conversations with a Norwegian merchant and an Anglo-Saxon trader to the Baltic show the king in the act of intelligence-gathering, further evidence of Alfred's hunger for new knowledge – Asser actually calls it the 'royal greed'.[64]

In writing of Alfred's inventiveness Asser also refers to him instructing goldsmiths and other craftsmen to produce 'wonderful and precious new treasures to his own design which far surpassed any tradition of his predecessors'.[65] It is possible that one of these treasures survives in the form of the so-called Alfred Jewel, which has the inscription around its base *Aelfred mec heht gewyrcan* – 'Alfred had me made'. The animal head which protrudes from the Jewel may once have held a pointer in ivory, antler or wood to trace out the words of a text for someone who was not very used to reading. It may even have been a new type of object designed by the king himself (possibly influenced by Jewish reading-pointers). What is particularly interesting is that the figure under the pear-drop-shaped rock crystal which forms the 'handle' of the Jewel has associations with Pope Gregory's text. The figure has very prominent eyes (there are parallels with the figure of Sight on another putative production of Alfred's royal workshop, the Fuller Brooch in the British Museum). Sight, of course, was necessary for reading and recalls Pope Gregory's stress on applying 'the eyes of the mind' to what one reads, of deliberating and mentally digesting it.

The Alfred Jewel is a work of the highest craftsmanship, made of gold and with its central figure created by enamelling (probably the work of one of the Frankish craftsmen whom Asser says the king employed). It was found during peat-digging in 1693 at North Petherton, close to the edge of the Somerset Levels, about 4 miles from Athelney, where Alfred hid from the Vikings and subsequently founded a monastery. There is the exciting possibility that the Jewel may once have belonged to the king himself, or to a senior person in his service; one imagines that its loss must have caused some disquiet.

A series of smaller *aestels* have also been recovered from different locations in England. Not all of these necessarily came from Alfred's royal workshops, but many of them do have features of decoration in common with the Alfred

Jewel, including fine enamel work and the use of gold that probably only royal patronage could have warranted. So it is possible that Alfred gave many of these pointers as gifts, as part of his desire to promote reading throughout his kingdom. As such they can be seen as a symbol of one of the distinctive features of his court. It is of particular interest that one such *aestel* has been found in a chieftain's hall in Borg in the Lofoten Islands of Norway, for Ohthere, the Norwegian merchant who gave Alfred an account of the geography of Scandinavia, seems to have been based on one of these islands.

Asser claims that Alfred spent a considerable part of his income on craftsmen. Many of the items they made would have been intended, like the *aestel*s, as gifts, for this was how kingship and overlordship were underpinned in the early Middle Ages. 'God loveth a cheerful giver',[66] proclaims Asser, and Alfred seems to have wanted to cultivate this quality in public (though God, in the form of the Anglo-Saxon Church, does not seem to be such a major beneficiary). A reputation for wealth and generosity attracted men to Alfred's service – Asser says he had many foreigners in his employ in army, churches and craftshops – and encouraged lesser kings to seek his patronage. Guthrum and Anarawd of Gwynedd were showered with gifts when they accepted Alfred's overlordship.

Asser devotes a whole chapter to the generous gifts he himself received from the king – which he seems to have had no qualms about accepting in spite of his criticisms of the wealth and lavish lifestyles of some Anglo-Saxon clergy. In addition to control of two major churches, Asser received a silk cloak and a quantity of incense weighing as much as a stout man, 'not to mention the countless daily gifts of worldly riches of every sort which it would be tedious to recount at this point for fear of boring my readers'.[67] Alfred's links with merchants such as Ohthere would have enabled him to acquire other rare and desirable commodities such as furs and walrus-tusk ivory, riches that could also be used to make his court a desirable destination and add value to acceptance of his lordship.

In terms of piety and religious belief Asser stresses the king's commitment to regular prayer, his attendance at Mass and devotion to the saints. Alfred certainly founded two religious houses and sent generous gifts to Rome. But the evidence from his will and land grants (or rather the lack of them) suggests he was not as generous towards the Church as Asser claims. The establishment of burhs and payment of his own military household may have made more pressing demands on Alfred's purse. There may be a certain element of wishful thinking in Asser's casting of Alfred as ideal Christian monarch. From this distance we can never know for certain the king's personal beliefs.

Alfred was in many ways a traditional Anglo-Saxon warrior king and overlord, and his promotion of the *Anglo-Saxon Chronicle* with its account of his victories over the Vikings was undoubtedly one of the ways he hoped to be remembered. Like Beowulf in the famous Old English poem, he would have wanted to leave behind him a reputation for bravery and generosity – two attributes of a 'good lord' in the poetic tradition on which he was brought up. It is this interest in marrying the heritage of Anglo-Saxon kingship with the insights of Christian learning that helps to make Alfred so distinctive and interesting – a ruthless military leader when necessary, but also reflective and aware of his moral responsibilities. Asser's Alfred may come over as too Christ-like for us to believe. We perhaps need to add into the mix a strong dash of Germanic heroism. The Saxons could be cunning and tricky as well as brave and inventive. The mysterious disappearance of King Ceolwulf II and the sidelining of his nephews may hint at a rather more devious side to Alfred, one that is usually concealed from us by his court scholars.

Alfred was inevitably constrained in what he could achieve. His kingdom was small and culturally marginal compared to the great Frankish realms, or even England in the following century. But his reign stands at the turning-point between the period of many small Anglo-Saxon kingdoms and the creation of a united country under his successors. It marks the moment when English came into its own as a written language. Alfred's support and example were crucial, as later Anglo-Saxons acknowledged, paving the way for the later high points of Anglo-Saxon Christian culture. If he had not stood firm against the Vikings and found the means to resist them, English history would be very different. There may not even have been an England.

Maps

Map 1: Britain at Alfred's birth, 848/9

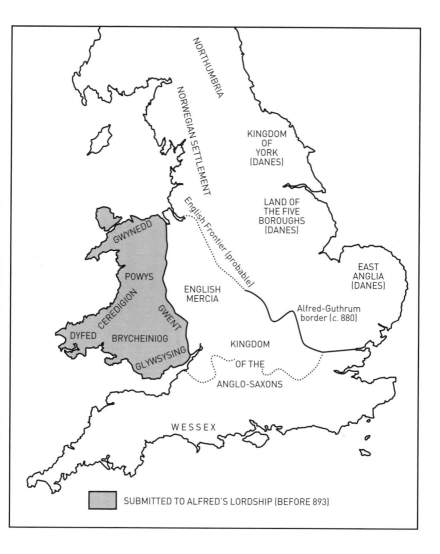

Map 2: Britain at Alfred's death, 899

Family Tree: Alfred and his family, and their Frankish connections

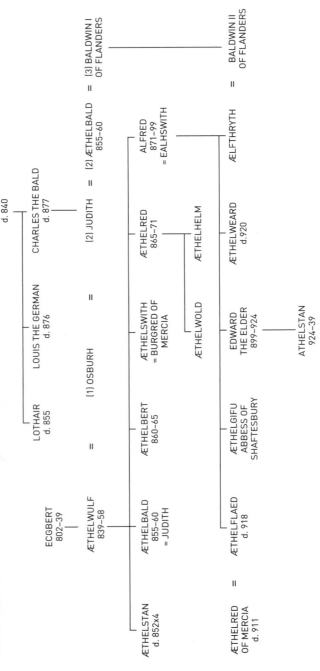

Notes

A Note about Sources

Many of the sources for Alfred's reign can be found in translation, either full or abstracted, in Keynes, Simon & Lapidge, Michael (eds), *Alfred the Great: Asser's* Life of King Alfred *and Other Contemporary Sources* (Penguin, 1983). Many of the same, and some additional sources, are contained in Whitelock, Dorothy (ed.), *English Historical Documents, Volume 1, c. 550–1042* (2nd edn, Eyre Methuen, 1979). Citations from the *Anglo-Saxon Chronicle* have been taken from this work, but a more easily obtainable translation is available in Swanton, Michael (ed.), *The Anglo-Saxon Chronicles* (Dent, 1996). Most of the 'events' described in the book come from the yearly entries in the *Anglo-Saxon Chronicle* and are not referenced separately.

1   Freeman, E., *The History of the Norman Conquest*, 6 vols, vol. I, p. 52 (Oxford, 1879).
2   Ibid., vol. I, p. 51.

3 Keynes, S. & Lapidge, M. (eds), *Alfred the Great: Asser's* Life of King Alfred *and Other Contemporary Sources* (Penguin, 1983), Asser chs 23–4.
4 Smyth, A.P., *King Alfred the Great* (Oxford University Press, 1995), pp. 149–367.
5 Keynes & Lapidge, *Alfred the Great*, Asser chs 99–102.
6 Ibid., Asser chs 124–6.
7 Keynes & Lapidge, *Alfred the Great*, ch. 22
8 Ibid., Asser ch. 17.
9 Ibid., Asser ch. 22.
10 Ibid., Asser ch. 74.
11 This is Osferth who was a beneficiary in Alfred's will and was a significant figure in the reigns of Alfred's son Edward and grandson Athelstan. In one charter of Edward's Osferth is described as 'the brother of the king'. See Keynes & Lapidge, *Alfred the Great*, p. 322 (where the attribution is dismissed as a 'mistake').
12 Keynes & Lapidge, *Alfred the Great*, Asser ch. 91.
13 Ibid., Asser ch. 75.
14 British Library Harley MS 2965; De Gray Birch, W., *An Ancient Manuscript of the Eighth or Ninth Century Formerly Belonging to St Mary's Abbey or Nunnaminster, Winchester* (Simpkin and Marshall, 1889).
15 Whitelock, D. (ed.), *English Historical Documents, Volume 1, c. 550–1042* (2nd edn, Eyre Methuen, 1979), pp. 879–80.
16 Keynes & Lapidge, *Alfred the Great*, Asser chs 37–9.
17 Ibid., pp. 193-4.

18 Keynes & Lapidge, *Alfred the Great*, Asser ch. 80.

19 Ibid., pp. 171–2.

20 Ibid., Asser chs 78–9.

21 Ibid., Asser ch. 80.

22 Ibid., Asser ch. 91.

23 Whitelock, *English Historical Documents*, p. 199.

24 Keynes & Lapidge, *Alfred the Great*, Asser ch. 83.

25 Ibid., pp. 171–2.

26 Ibid., Asser ch. 101, see also chs 93–4.

27 King Alfred's address to his bishops, Keynes & Lapidge, *Alfred the Great*, p. 126.

28 Keynes & Lapidge, *Alfred the Great*, Asser ch. 91.

29 Ibid., pp. 124–6.

30 Ibid., pp. 173–8.

31 Ibid., Asser chs 92–8.

32 Ibid., Asser ch. 102.

33 Whitelock, *English Historical Documents* pp. 881–3.

34 Keynes & Lapidge, *Alfred the Great*, pp. 182–6.

35 Ibid., Asser chs 78–9, 88–9.

36 Ibid., 124–6.

37 III Kings 3:11–14; II Chronicle 1, 7–12; Pratt, D., *The Political Thought of King Alfred the Great* (Cambridge University Press, 2007),pp. 150–66.

38 Keynes & Lapidge, *Alfred the Great*, Asser ch. 91.

39 Ibid., Asser ch. 75.

40 Ibid., Asser ch. 106.

41 Whitelock, *English Historical Documents*, pp.,206.

42 Keynes & Lapidge, *Alfred the Great*, Asser ch. 91.

43 Ibid., pp. 173–8.

44 Mynors, R.A.B., Thomson, R.M. & Winterbottom, M., *William of Malmesbury, Gesta Regum Anglorum* I (Clarendon Press, 1998), pp. 210–11.

45 Keynes & Lapidge, *Alfred the Great*, pp. 174–5.

46 Ibid., pp. 189–91.

47 Ibid., pp. 197–202.

48 Mynors, Thomson & Winterbottom, *William of Malmesbury*, pp. 182–5.

49 Ibid., pp. 206–9.

50 Freeman, *Norman Conquest*, vol. I, p. 51.

51 Manning, E., *Marble and Bronze: The Art and Life of Hamo Thornycroft* (Trefoil Books, 1982), pp. 144–5.

52 Yorke, B., *The King Alfred Millenary in Winchester, 1901* (Hampshire Papers 17, 1999).

53 Bowker, A., *The King Alfred Millenary* (Macmillan, 1902), pp. 126–7.

54 Ibid., pp. 119–21.

55 Ibid., p. 21.

56 Keynes & Lapidge, *Alfred the Great*, Asser ch. 76

57 Whitelock, *English Historical Documents*, pp. 544–6.

58 Keynes & Lapidge, *Alfred the Great*, Asser chs 105–6.

59 Attenborough, F.L,, *The Laws of the Earliest English Kings* (Cambridge University Press, 1922), pp. 62–94, ch. 13.

60 Keynes & Lapidge, *Alfred the Great*, Asser ch. 76.

61 Ibid., Asser ch. 91.

62 Ibid., Asser chs 103–4.

63 Lavelle, R., *Alfred's Wars: Sources and Interpretations of Anglo-Saxon Warfare in the Viking Age* (Boydell Press, 2010), pp. 92–4.

64 Keynes & Lapidge, *Alfred the Great*, Asser ch. 78.

65 Ibid., Asser chs 76 and 101.

66 Ibid., Asser ch. 101; II Corinthians ix, 7.

67 Keynes & Lapidge, *Alfred the Great*, Asser, ch. 81.

Glossary

Anglo-Saxon	name derived from two major Germanic groups to be established in Britain, the Angles and Saxons; applied to the period *c.* 400–1066
alms	charitable payment, e.g. to a religious body
annal	yearly entry in a chronicle
bretwalda	term applied to great Anglo-Saxon overlords listed in *Anglo-Saxon Chronicle* entry for 825; may mean 'ruler of Britain' or 'broad ruler'
British	name applied to Welsh-speaking native inhabitants of Britain
burhs	defensive sites, such as those erected or refurbished by King Alfred against the Vikings
Carolingian Renaissance	major revival of Church and culture in ninth-century Francia
charters	records of grants of land
ealdorman	noble delegated by the king to have charge of a shire and lead its forces in battle

Francia	homeland of the Franks, consisting not only of modern France, but also much of Austria, Germany, the Low Countries, Switzerland, and in the ninth century much of Italy as well
hide	Anglo-Saxon measurement of land, also used for assessing liability to public services
Mercia	Anglo-Saxon Midland kingdom occupying land between the rivers Thames and Humber
reeve	royal official, typically with responsibility for the management of royal estates or towns
shires	main administrative subdivisions of Wessex, supervised by ealdormen. After the Norman Conquest the term 'county' was applied to these units; pre-1974 county boundaries were very close to those of the Anglo-Saxon shires in Wessex.
Viking	Name applied to groups composed primarily of Danes and Norwegians who raided and settled in Britain in the ninth and tenth centuries
Wessex	Anglo-Saxon kingdom based south of the Thames
witan	the royal counsel of 'wise men'

Timeline

It is not always possible to date events in the Anglo-Saxon period accurately or assign them to a particular year, so the following conventions should be noted: 848/49 indicates that the event occurred in one or other of those years, but we do not know which (a complicating fact is that not all Anglo-Saxon written texts began their year on 1 January). 890x892 indicates that the event took place at some point within the stated timeframe; *c.* (i.e. *circa*) 885 indicates a greater uncertainty about when an event occurred.

848/49	Birth of Alfred at Wantage
853	First visit of Alfred to Rome
855	Second visit of Alfred to Rome with his father King Æthelwulf
856	Æthelwulf marries Charles's daughter Judith; revolt of Æthelwulf's oldest surviving son Æthelbald; Æthelwulf retires to eastern Wessex
858	Death of Æthelwulf
860	Death of Æthelbald; accession of Æthelbert to the whole of Wessex
865	Viking army overwinters in Thanet

866	Death of Æthelbert; accession of Æthelred
868	Siege of Nottingham; marriage of Alfred to Ealhswith
870	King Edmund of East Angles killed by Vikings
871	Battle of Ashdown; death of Æthelred; accession of Alfred
874	Exile of King Burgred of Mercia; succession of Ceolwulf II
876	Vikings occupy Wareham and Exeter
878	Alfred withdraws to Athelney; Battle of Edington; defeated Guthrum converts to Christianity
879	Guthrum occupies Cirencester; disappearance of Ceolwulf II; new Viking army at Fulham
880	Guthrum becomes king in East Anglia; Fulham army returns to continent
***c.* 880x893**	Foundation of religious houses in Athelney and Shaftesbury
885	Siege of Rochester; Alfred's sends naval force to East Anglia; Alfred meets Asser
886	Restoration of London; submission of all the English people not under Danish rule to Alfred
***c.* 886**	arrival of Grimbald from Francia; marriage of Alfred's oldest daughter Æthelflaed to Æthelred of Mercia
887	Asser joins Alfred's court permanently
890	Death of Guthrum

c. **890**	Completion and circulation of Old English translation of Gregory's *Pastoral Care*; writing of Alfred's law code
890x892	Completion and circulation of *Anglo-Saxon Chronicle*
892	Arrival of Viking forces commanded by Hastein
893x899	Marriage of Alfred's daughter Ælfthryth to Baldwin II of Flanders
893	Asser writes his biography of Alfred; siege of Exeter; other Vikings kept on the move by Æthelred of Mercia; Vikings overwinter in Chester
894	Vikings in Wales and retreat to Mersea (Essex); others from siege of Exeter defeated near Chichester
c. **894**	Birth of Alfred's grandson Athelstan
895	Alfred defends London; Vikings withdraw to Bridgnorth
896	Viking force disperses; Alfred designs new longships
899	26 October: Death of King Alfred; burial in Old Minster, Winchester
901	foundation of New Minster, Winchester; Alfred's body transferred

Further Reading

Abels, Richard, *Alfred the Great: War, Kingship and Culture in Anglo-Saxon England* (Longman, 1998)

Bately, Janet & Englert, Anton (eds), *Ohthere's Voyages: A Late 9th-Century Account of Voyages Along the Coasts of Norway and Denmark and its Cultural Context* (Roskilde Viking Ship Museum, 2007)

Blackburn, Mark & Dumville, David (eds), *Kings, Currency and Alliances: History and Coinage of Southern England in the Ninth Century* (Boydell Press, 1998)

Godden, Malcolm & Irvine, Susan (eds), *The Old English Boethius: An Edition of the Old English Version of Boethius's* De Consolatione Philosophiae (2 vols, Oxford University Press, 2009)

Hadley, Dawn, The *Vikings in England: Settlement, Society and Culture* (Manchester University Press, 2006)

Higham, Nicholas & Ryan, Martin J., *The Anglo-Saxon World* (Yale University Press, 2013)

Hill, David & Rumble, Alexander (eds), *The Defence of Wessex: The Burghal Hidage and Anglo-Saxon Fortifications* (Manchester University Press, 1996)

Hinton, David, *The Alfred Jewel and Other Late Saxon Decorated Metalwork* (Ashmolean Museum, 2008)

Horspool, David, *Why Alfred Burned the Cakes: A King and his Eleven-Hundred-Year Afterlife* (Profile, 2006)

Kershaw, Paul, 'Illness, Power and Prayer in Asser's *Life of King Alfred*', *Early Medieval Europe*, 10 (2001), pp. 201–24

Keynes, Simon, 'The Cult of King Alfred the Great', *Anglo-Saxon England*, 28 (1999), pp. 225–356

Keynes, Simon & Lapidge, Michael (eds), *Alfred the Great. Asser's* Life of King Alfred *and Other Contemporary Sources* (Penguin, 1983)

Lavelle, Ryan, *Alfred's Wars: Sources and Interpretations of Anglo-Saxon Warfare in the Viking Age* (Boydell Press, 2010)

Pratt, David, *The Political Thought of King Alfred the Great* (Cambridge University Press, 2007)

Reuter, Timothy (ed.), *Alfred the Great: Papers from the Eleventh-Centenary Conferences* (Ashgate, 2003)

Smyth, Alfred P., *King Alfred the Great* (Oxford University Press, 1995)

Swanton, Michael (ed.), *The Anglo-Saxon Chronicles* (Dent, 1996)

Whitelock, Dorothy (ed.), *English Historical Documents, Volume 1, c. 550–1042* (2nd edn, Eyre Methuen, 1979)

Williams, Gareth, *Early Anglo-Saxon Coins* (Shire Archaeology, 2008)

Yorke, Barbara, *Wessex in the Early Middle Ages* (Leicester University Press, 1995)

Web Links

There are limited sites devoted to Alfred, but rather more good early medieval ones with some material for Alfred or wider background material.

www.ogdoad.force9.co.uk/alfred/alfredintro.htm –
Webpages on King Alfred on the Anglo-Saxon England Web-Ring

http://britisharchaeology.ashmus.ox.ac.uk/highlights/ alfred-jewel.html – The Alfred Jewel at the Ashmolean Museum

www.winchester.ac.uk/searchforalfred – University of Winchester – Webpages on the Saxon bones from Hyde Abbey

www.fitzmuseum.cam.ac.uk/dept/coins/emc – The Fitzwilliam Museum's searchable database of coin finds

www.kemble.asnc.cam.ac.uk – Anglo-Saxon charters website

www.pase.ac.uk – Searchable biographical database for Anglo-Saxons

www.heroicage.org – Online journal on early middle ages with many useful weblinks

POCKET GIANTS **ALFRED THE GREAT**

www.anglo-saxons.net – A general site on Anglo-Saxons, with further links

www.medievalists.net – General news site for medievalists with many useful links